MW00451542

To my twin sister, Lauren, who inspired me to get out of my comfort zone to travel the world and encouraged me to move to Bali. This chapter of my life really shaped this entire book!

And to my husband, Alex, who is essentially the second author of this book. It was truly a joint effort and I could not have done it without you.

THE

Global

VEGAN

ELLIE BULLEN

plum.

Pan Macmillan Australia

CONTENTS

INTRODUCTION

Hello! My name is Ellie. Some of you may know me from my plant-based recipe blog and Instagram account, Elsa's Wholesome Life. I published my first book in 2017 and I am very excited to be back with even more delicious vegan recipes, inspired by the incredible cuisines from countries I have visited in my travels.

But first, a little bit about myself! I grew up in Lennox Head, a small Australian beachside town that is close to beautiful forests and lush farmland. Growing up in this special part of the world really gave me an appreciation for a healthy and active lifestyle and I developed an interest in wholesome food from an early age. I became passionate about cooking and holistic health, and this lead me to study in this field at university. I am now proud to say that I am a qualified dietitian and nutritionist.

Along the way, I started my blog because I wanted to share my experience and teach others how to live a wholesome life, too. There is a lot of noise in the nutrition area these days and my aim has always been to provide clear information about a plant-based diet, as well as simple, well-balanced vegan meals. Aside from cooking classes overseas, everything I have learned in the kitchen has been completely self-taught, and I love creating delicious recipes that I know people will easily be able to make at home.

Alongside food and wellness, my other big passion is travel! Earlier this year, my husband and I moved back to Australia after living in Bali. We absolutely loved living overseas. Not only did it bring us many new experiences, allow us to make new friends and challenge us, it also helped us appreciate our home back in Australia. Living immersed in another culture gave me a greater respect for different ways of living, allowing me to be more open-minded about alternative food beliefs. I also learned a lot about different ingredients and cuisines along the way.

We lived in Bali for just over two years and used our home as a base from which to travel the world. Since writing my first cookbook, we have visited more than 20 countries across South East Asia, the Middle East, Europe, the South Pacific and North America. I am incredibly grateful to have been able to see and experience so many places already. Travelling teaches you many new lessons and life skills. Of course, with my passion for cooking, I was excited to try out new ingredients and take inspiration from local dishes that I could come home and 'vegan-ise'.

One thing that I often do when visiting a new country is book into a cooking class. It's a wonderful way to meet locals, tour markets, discover new ingredients and learn how to cook some local dishes. It's also usually a great laugh! I love hearing a local explain each ingredient and the correct way to prepare it, as well as talking about their culture and traditions – you really do learn so much!

Of course, following a plant-based diet can be pretty difficult when travelling and it was one of the biggest challenges for me, but I did learn to be more patient, respectful and accepting of other cultures and lifestyles. There were definitely times along the way where my diet wasn't the most wholesome due to the plant-based options being so limited, and this was difficult. On the other hand, I was very pleased to see how plant-based eating is gaining popularity around the world. You may be surprised to learn that Indonesia (mainly Bali) and Mexico (Tulum) have some of the best vegan food I have ever eaten!

The cooking classes I took in various countries were some of my favourite travel experiences. In Vietnam I learned about the different aromatic herbs and spices used in their cuisine, and visited the local farms by bicycle to pick organic greens and herbs. I really enjoyed wandering through the markets in South Korea and learning about the traditional Chinese medicines used there. It was incredible to experience the mix of smells from the herbs, fermenting vegetables and seafood. In Mexico I was inspired by the freshness of the ingredients and the wholesomeness and flavour of the dishes. Finally, living in Indonesia I learned so much, including how to cook with tempeh and jackfruit. These have become two of my favourite ingredients and I now incorporate them into recipes from other cuisines.

After so many amazing foodie experiences overseas, I have been bursting to share what I have learned with you! This book features recipes that are inspired by the places I have visited, including Indonesia, India, Vietnam, Thailand, Mexico, the United States, Greece, Italy, Turkey, Portugal and the Middle East. You'll find loads of vegan takes on well-loved classics, such as pad Thai, moussaka, caesar salad and even fried eggs! There are wholesome brekkies, satisfying meals for any time of day and mouth-watering sweets, as well as smoothies, shakes and other nourishing drinks. As with all of my food, these recipes are packed full of vegetables, fruits and herbs, alongside plenty of whole grains, legumes, nuts, seeds and healthy oils.

I have also included a section on plant-based nutrition (see page 13), which looks at key nutrients and how to ensure you are getting enough of them, as well as a glossary of my favourite ingredients (see page 20) where I talk about some of the ingredients I have discovered in my travels that have now become pantry staples for me.

I hope you enjoy cooking the recipes in *The Global Vegan* as much as I enjoyed creating them. I am so excited for you to get into the kitchen to try them out – and hopefully feel like you are travelling along with me to some of these beautiful and exotic countries!

x Ellie

WHY A PLANT-BASED DIET?

FOR HEALTH

Quite simply, a diet rich in vegetables, legumes, whole grains, fruits, nuts and seeds is amazing for your health and vitality. Together, these foods have plenty of carbohydrates for energy, fibre for digestion and gut micro biome, healthy unsaturated fats, complete plant protein, as well as heaps of vitamins and minerals, including crucial nutrients such as vitamin C, folate, zinc and magnesium.

In 2019, a new Canadian food guide was released and it is an excellent example of how governments can promote a more plant-based lifestyle. The visual guide shows a plate, where animal products and sugar have been reduced; the meat and dairy food groups have been removed; plant and animal protein sources are grouped into 'protein foods'; and fruit and vegetables together take up half of the plate. The new guide advises 'among protein foods, consume plant-based more often'.

When embarking on any diet, you must educate yourself in order to make it work for you. If you cannot make it work 100 per cent of the time that's okay, because I strongly believe in the philosophy of progress over perfection, and any improvement, small or large, is a step in the right direction!

FOR THE PLANET

The livestock industry is one of the biggest contributors to environmental damage today. This includes pollution, water use, land use, species extinction, antibiotic resistance and fish species depletion. Raising animals for meat and dairy products requires enormous amounts of land to grow their feed, which in turn requires irrigation/water use. To produce 1 kg of beef, up to 13 kg of grain and 15,000 litres of water is used. This is a huge amount of grain that we could be using to feed the world, and land we could use to farm other food sources. Livestock also contributes to climate change due to the methane gas produced by cows and other grazing animals.

MAXIMISING KEY VITAMINS & MINERALS

While a plant-based diet is really wholesome, there are a few nutrients that are particularly important and you need to make sure you are getting the right amounts.

Iron

Iron is an important mineral involved in red blood cell formation, oxygen transport around our tissues and organs, maintaining energy levels, and mood stabilisation.

Iron deficiency is the most common nutrient deficiency in the world and adequate iron intake is particularly important for women with a monthly cycle. Getting enough iron from a plant-based diet can be challenging since non-haem iron (iron that comes from plant sources) is less bio-available (less absorbable) so it's important to focus on getting enough in your diet by following the steps below, or simply take a good-quality iron supplement.

Iron requirements:
Men: 9 mg/day
Women: 18 mg/day
Pregnant women: 27 mg/day.

Iron-rich plant-based foods include:
- legumes (beans, peas, lentils)
- nuts and seeds
- soy products (milk, tofu, tempeh)
- grains
- dark leafy green vegetables (spinach, silverbeet, broccoli, bok choy and kale).

How to improve the bio-availability of non-haem iron:

1. Eat iron-rich foods with vitamin C–rich foods, such as tomatoes, sweet potatoes, citrus fruits and berries, as vitamin C assists iron absorption.

2. Soak your grains, legumes, nuts and seeds overnight to break down the phytates. In our bodies, phytic acid tends to bind to minerals such as iron, zinc and calcium, making them less bio-available.

3. Consume small amounts of iron-rich foods across the whole day, as your body doesn't absorb large, single doses well.

4. Have regular blood tests with your GP (every three to six months) and if your levels are too low, consider an iron supplement or infusion.

Vitamin B12

This vitamin plays an important role in red blood cell formation, brain and nervous system function and DNA replication, but can only be found in animal foods (meat, eggs, dairy), even though you may find some misleading information about B12 being found in foods such as spirulina, tempeh and mushrooms. This means those following a plant-based diet are at risk of developing a deficiency in vitamin B12, which can cause symptoms such as fatigue, nervous system damage and digestive issues, as well as neurological problems such as depression and memory loss.

Therefore, an exclusively vegan diet must include some food sources that have been fortified with vitamin B12 or supplements. My favourite food form is nutritional yeast, which I add to dips and sauces or sprinkle on my dinners. Some store-bought cereals and veggie patties are also fortified with B12 – check the ingredients label.

This is another nutrient that you'll need to keep track of with your GP or dietitian, and consider taking as a supplement if your levels are too low. When supplementing vitamin B12, look for cyanocobalamin since it can be converted to both types of B12 in the body, or a supplement that contains both types that the body uses (methylcobalamin and adenosylcobalamin).

Calcium

Calcium is a crucial mineral for maintaining strong bones, efficient muscular contractions (including your heart!), nerve signalling and blood clotting. A healthy amount of calcium in your blood is vital, and your body will forfeit calcium from your bone stores if you are not getting enough.

The main dietary source of calcium is dairy foods and small bony fish, such as sardines. I have listed the plant foods that are richest in calcium below. Some plant-based milks are fortified with calcium, and you may like to fortify homemade nut milks with calcium supplements. I do this rather than take a supplement, as nutrients are best absorbed when consumed with other nutrients at mealtimes across the day. It is also important to note that calcium and iron compete for binding and therefore absorption, so try to consume calcium-rich foods/supplements separately from iron-rich foods.

Calcium-rich plant-based foods include:
- leafy green vegetables
- nuts and seeds
- fortified cereals, non-dairy milks and tofu.

Zinc

Zinc is required for immune system function, cell division, cell growth, wound healing and carbohydrate metabolism.

Since the richest sources of zinc include beef, pork, lamb, shellfish and oysters, a vegetarian or vegan diet is at risk of being low. Also, similarly to calcium and iron, the phytates in legumes and grains inhibit the absorption of the zinc within them and therefore cooked, sprouted, soaked and fermented variations can improve bio-availability.

Zinc-rich plant-based foods include:
- nuts
- seeds such as hemp, sesame and pumpkin
- whole grains
- legumes
- yeast
- dark chocolate.

MACRONUTRIENTS

Macronutrients are the nutrients we need in the largest amounts – carbohydrates, proteins and fats.

Carbohydrates

Many people think the term 'carbs' refers to foods like bread and pasta, and that we shouldn't eat them. But carbohydrates are actually found in almost every food except meat and eggs. They're in grains, fruits, vegetables, nuts, seeds and even dairy products, and are the preferred fuel for our brains and bodies. We just need to learn to eat the right kinds of carbs and in the right amounts.

Carbohydrates are sometimes grouped into 'simple' and 'complex'. Simple carbs, commonly known as sugars, are small molecules; they are digested and absorbed quickly into the bloodstream, which can cause rapid spikes in blood sugar. Foods high in sugar are typically packaged foods like soft drinks, chocolates, confectionary, biscuits, cakes and pies, as well as sauces, condiments and sweeteners. These have what is known as a high glycaemic index (GI) and, depending on how much of them you eat, they can also have a high glycaemic load (GL).

There are two main types of complex carbs: starches and fibre. Starches are found in vegetables, such as potato, sweet potato and sweet corn, and in grains, such as oats, wheat, rice and rye. While starches take longer for the body to break down and therefore provide longer lasting energy, they are also eventually converted to glucose.

Fibre, on the other hand, is the name given to the parts of plants that are resistant to digestion in the small intestine so they hang around the colon, where they bulk up our stools and help to feed friendly bacteria.

There are two types of fibre: insoluble and soluble. Insoluble fibre helps build up your number twos, while soluble fibre attracts water into the colon and helps soften your stools, so they exit more easily. Basically, fibre is great for keeping your bowels regular and healthy. Fibre in food also slows digestion, helping to delay spikes in your blood glucose, as well as trapping fats from being absorbed. Processed grains, such as white rice and white flour, have had the outer layer of bran removed, which means they have less fibre and more starch and are quickly converted to glucose in the body. This is why I prefer to eat whole grains, such as oats and brown rice.

No matter how you dress it up, too much sugar of any kind is not good for your body. It doesn't matter if it's fructose-free, unrefined or highly refined – it's still sugar. And unless you need that sugar for a bout of intense exercise, it's going to get stored as fat or hang around the body and mess with your insulin levels.

Protein

Protein is important, not only for building muscle but also for growing our hair and nails, making enzymes and hormones, and even making our red blood cells.

Our bodies break down all the protein we eat into amino acids (I like to think of them as little building blocks), which are then used to grow and repair tissues and to create the enzymes and hormones we need for digestion and myriad other functions. There are 21 different amino acids, nine of which are essential, meaning our bodies cannot synthesise them from other amino acids and we must get them from our diet.

So where do I get my protein from? The answer is legumes (peas, beans and peanuts), nuts, grains and seeds, all of which contain plant protein. All we need to do is to eat a good variety and quantity of these foods. I pair my legumes, such as lentils, with a grain, such as rice. That way I know I'm getting all nine essential amino acids since they contain different types of essential amino acids. This is known as a 'complete protein' source. Hemp and quinoa are two plant-based foods that are complete protein sources, so I like to include them in my diet daily.

Fats

Eating healthy fats as part of every meal is really important. Our bodies need fats. In fact, every single cell inside your body has a surface layer of fats, and since we are constantly replacing our cells an intake of fats is essential. Fats help to keep your skin and hair healthy and also help you to absorb fat-soluble vitamins A, D, E and K from your food.

The general consensus has always been that saturated fats (found in meat, dairy and some plant oils, such as coconut and palm oil) are considered 'bad', and unsaturated fats (from plants, nuts and seeds) are considered 'good'. This is because saturated fats are more readily stored as fat in the body and less easily used as fuel, leading to raised levels of bad cholesterol (LDL), which in turn can lead to fatty deposits in your blood vessels and an increased risk of cardiovascular disease.

There are two types of unsaturated fats: monounsaturated and polyunsaturated. Monounsaturated fats are abundant in olive oil, avocado, almonds, cashews, macadamias and eggs. These fats raise the levels of good cholesterol (HDL) in your blood, decreasing your risk of heart disease, which means they should be enjoyed as part of a balanced diet.

Polyunsaturated fats are found in seeds and seed oils (sunflower, safflower, flaxseed, sesame), legume oils (soybean and peanut), fish and walnuts. Two types of polyunsaturated fats, omega-3 and omega-6, are known as essential fatty acids, and it's worth looking at them in greater detail.

As a rule of thumb, I live by the motto 'less 6, more 3'. Yes, there are two types of dietary omega fatty acids: 3 and 6. These are essential, meaning we cannot make them in our body and require these from the diet. Omega-3 and omega-6 compete for the same enzyme in our bodies, and omega-6 is highly available in our modern diet (in processed foods, seed and vegetable oils, for example). An imbalanced ratio of omega-6 and omega-3 is linked to increased heart attacks, depression, obesity and cancer; therefore consciously decreasing our intake of omega-6 is advised as opposed to guzzling down as much omega-3 fatty acids as we can. The correct ratio of omega-3 to omega-6 is 1:2, yet a Western diet that is high in processed foods is more like 1:20.

While nuts and seeds contain a higher ratio of omega-6 to omega-3, avoidance of these whole foods is not advised since they also contain fibre, protein and micronutrients and a handful a day has been shown to reduce your risk of heart disease. Instead, try to avoid processed foods and takeaway foods with vegetable and seed oils, and opt for healthy oils when cooking, such as avocado, olive and macadamia.

Interestingly, omega-3 fatty acids in fish actually come from the micro-algae that they eat, so we can get this nutrient straight from the source! While food sources of micro-algae are not very common, there are now algae DHA supplements readily available. With the seafood industry being highly unsustainable, algae may be a more environmentally friendly option as well.

MY FAVOURITE INGREDIENTS

Here is the lowdown on some of my favourite plant-based ingredients – items that I always keep in my pantry or fridge to add flavour, texture and nutrition to my meals. Keep these on hand to easily whip up any of the delicious dishes in this book.

AQUAFABA

Aquafaba is the liquid in canned chickpeas that is often poured right out of the can and down the drain. When I first learned about this I thought it was a really strange concept as I found chickpea water a little bit stinky. However, aquafaba is a great egg white substitute and this is a great way to use this otherwise discarded ingredient! You may see it replace eggs in vegan cocktails, meringues and aioli or mayo.

BEETROOT POWDER

Beetroot powder is a great way to naturally colour foods bright pink. It is made by dehydrating beetroot and grinding it into a powder. Beetroot is high in folate and vitamin C (which supports collagen networks).

BESAN FLOUR

Besan flour is made from chickpeas and is high in protein and gluten free. It is commonly used in Indian cuisine to make bread.

CALCIUM SUPPLEMENTS

Calcium supplements can be used to boost the calcium in homemade plant-based milks and other vegan dishes. I do this rather than take a supplement, as nutrients are best absorbed when consumed with other nutrients at mealtimes across the day.

CHIA SEEDS

These seeds are packed with nutrition. They contain all nine essential amino acids, and have a fantastic fat profile, high in omega-3 fatty acids. They're also high in fibre and make a great egg replacement in dishes as they soak up the liquid and become gelatinous. My favourite way to have them is in my keto bircher (see page 38).

CHIPOTLE SAUCE

Chipotle is actually a jalapeño chilli that has been smoke-dried, hence the smoky flavour. This smoky dried chilli powder is mixed with spices, vinegar, salt, sugar and tomatoes to make a chipotle sauce. I use a store-bought chipotle sauce that I find in the Mexican section of fine foods stores.

COCONUT AMINOS

Coconut aminos is a soy-free sweet sauce that tastes a bit like kecap manis. It's made from fermented coconut nectar and salt and is sometimes flavoured with chilli, garlic and onion. It is seriously my favourite sauce right now, I love it on almost anything, even just as a dressing on a salad.

COCONUT NECTAR

Coconut nectar is the sap from the coconut palm. I love using it in place of sugar as a natural syrup sweetener because it has a delicious caramel flavour.

DRIED WAKAME

Wakame is a type of edible seaweed. I add the dried version to dishes in this book such as my vegan fish sauce (see page 275) and fysh and chips (see page 185) as it adds a fishy umami flavour. You can find it in health-food stores and Asian grocers.

ERYTHRITOL POWDER

Erythritol powder is a low-calorie sweetener that belongs to the sugar alcohol group, or polyols, found naturally in small amounts in some fruits and vegetables. It is produced via yeast fermentation of glucose in vegetables such as corn or wheat.

FLAX SEEDS

Flax seeds are another seed I love to include in my daily diet. I use ground flax meal in some recipes as an egg replacement. In a similar way to chia seeds, it absorbs water and takes on a gelatinous egg-like texture. Flax seeds are high in omega-3 fatty acids.

GALANGAL

Galangal is actually part of the ginger family or more technically, rhizomes. In Thailand I learned about cooking with galangal and they actually called it 'Thai ginger'. Galangal has a pale, tough skin and a different flavour to ginger which could be described as earthy, citrusy and piney. It is usually sliced and steeped in soups rather than grated.

GOCHUJANG

Gochujang is a Korean fermented chilli paste that is slightly sweet and spicy. I learned about gochujang in South Korea and use it in a handful of my Korean dishes. You can find it in Asian supermarket or online.

HEMP SEEDS

Hemp seeds are the seed of the cannabis/hemp plant. They do not contain THC (the principal psychoactive constituent of cannabis) and they are legal here in Australia. I visited a hemp farm just prior to harvest and learned all about this super plant and super food. Hemp seeds are rich in protein and omega-3 fatty acids. I try to eat 1 tablespoon daily, sprinkled over almost any sweet or savoury dish!

JACKFRUIT

Native to South West India but also commonly found across South East Asia, jackfruit comes from the jack tree, which is in the fig, mulberry and breadfruit family. In my dishes, only young or green (unripe) jackfruit is used as when cooked into savoury dishes it takes on a 'pulled pork' texture and soaks up delicious sauces. You can find canned young jackfruit in many health-food stores as well as in supermarkets.

KAKADU PLUM POWDER

Kakadu plum (gubinge) is a native Australian fruit with a rich history as a bush food and medicine going back thousands of years. The powder is made from the dried and ground fruits and is very high in vitamin C.

KALA NAMAK (HIMALAYAN BLACK SALT)

Kala namak, also known as Himalayan black salt, is used in South Asia and has a sulphurous, egg-like smell and flavour. It is from the salts mined in the regions surrounding the Himalayas and is composed largely of sodium chloride with several other components, including sulphur, lending the salt its colour and smell. When ground into a powder, its colour ranges from purple to pink. I use kala namak in my vegan 'egg' dishes (see pages 44, 46 and 49).

KIMCHI

Kimchi is a popular fermented vegetable condiment originating from South Korea. It is made using cabbage, carrots, onion, garlic, ginger, Korean chilli powder, salt and sugar, and traditionally, shrimp paste and fish sauce are also used. It is fermented via lacto-fermentation, resulting in a rich, sour probiotic condiment, a little like sauerkraut. I have included a brilliant recipe for kimchi in this book (see page 284).

KONJAC NOODLES

Konjac noodles (shirataki) are thin, transparent Japanese noodles made from the konjac yam. Konjac consists of a type of soluble fibre called glucomannan, so these noodles are mostly indigestible and very low-calorie. Typically, they are touted as a diet food, but they also make for a high-fibre alternative to pasta or noodles. While experimenting with konjac noodles I discovered that their stretchy texture made them a great calamari substitute.

LIQUID SMOKE

Liquid smoke is used to add a wood-smoke flavour to dishes – think BBQ-Tex-Mex. Small amounts of liquid smoke are safe to consume. You can find it in specialty stores or online.

LIQUID STEVIA

Liquid stevia is an extract from the stevia leaf, a herb native to South America. It is used as a sugar-free sweetener. Although pure dried stevia has a pretty awful aftertaste, I have found that the liquid extracts add sweetness to dishes without that aftertaste.

NUTRITIONAL YEAST FLAKES

Nutritional yeast flakes are deactivated yeast that is often fortified with vitamin B12. It is different to both baker's yeast and brewer's yeast as it is deactivated so it will not rise or bubble. Nutritional yeast has a savoury, almost cheesy, flavour so is often added to vegan cheeses or sauces. It can also be sprinkled over salads and added to patties and pasta sauces.

QUINOA

Quinoa is my favourite high-protein whole grain. It is actually a seed but has a nutritional profile closer to a grain and originates from South America. It contains all nine essential amino acids, is gluten free and high in fibre. It comes in black, white and red but I often buy the tri-colour quinoa. It is quick to cook, so it's great to have on hand for a speedy dinner.

REISHI MUSHROOM POWDER

Reishi is a herbal and medicinal mushroom with a bitter taste. It is used for its immune boosting potential and to treat viral infections such as the flu. Research on its use in medicine is still early. I discovered this herbal mushroom on my travels to the United States where it is gaining popularity in the health food world. I use reishi and other herbal mushrooms in the plant protein blends that I developed for my store.

SAMBAL OELEK

Sambal oelek is an Indonesian chilli sauce or paste made from a variety of chillies, garlic, ginger, vinegar, palm sugar, lime and sometimes shrimp paste. It is readily found in supermarkets and Asian grocers. I enjoy adding it to any Asian dish for extra spice or in place of sriracha or gochujang.

SPIRULINA

Spirulina is a type of blue-green algae that is dried into a powder and added as a dietary supplement as it is a rich source of iron. It is a rich green colour and is often added to smoothies and juices.

TAMARIND PASTE

This sour, tangy paste made from the tamarind plant is similar to a date paste but less sweet and tangier. It is very common in Thai cuisine, notably in pad thai. You can find tamarind paste in supermarkets and Asian grocers.

TEMPEH

Tempeh is an excellent plant-based protein source. It is made from the fermentation of soy beans and is a less processed, healthier version of tofu. It is rich in both protein and fibre as well as many vitamins and minerals. Tempeh is traditionally made in Indonesia and my favourite way to cook it is to slice it thinly, marinate it in coconut aminos and then pan fry.

TEXTURED VEGETABLE PROTEIN (TVP)

Textured vegetable protein (also known as textured soy protein) is made from de-fatted soy flour in the process of making soy bean oil. It is high in protein and often used as a meat replacement as, when cooked, it resembles the texture of minced beef. It is commonly used in veggie spaghetti, pies, tacos or hamburger patties. Since it is more processed than organic tofu and tempeh I tend to use TVP only occasionally, but its resemblance to minced meat makes it very useful in dishes such as my spaghetti bolognese.

INDONESIAN CRUMPETS

These crumpets are inspired by childhood memories (I grew up on crumpets smothered in butter and honey!) and my time living in Bali, where apam balik – an Indonesian street-food dessert – has a similar texture to crumpets. This vegan version whisks me right back to those times, and while this delicious breakfast might be a slight labour of love to create, it is definitely worth it.

Makes about 20
250 ml (1 cup) soy or
   coconut milk
7 g sachet dried active yeast
1 teaspoon coconut sugar
300 g (2 cups) plain flour
2 teaspoons bicarbonate of soda
1 teaspoon sea salt
1 teaspoon vanilla powder
olive oil or vegan butter,
   for greasing

Suggested toppings
Coconut Yoghurt (see page 264)
vegan butter
pure maple syrup
fresh berries
shredded basil leaves
dried edible flowers
hemp seeds
icing sugar

Gently warm the soy or coconut milk and 250 ml (1 cup) of water in a saucepan over low heat until just warmed through (don't warm the liquid too much or you will kill your yeast). Pour the liquid into a bowl and add the dried yeast and sugar. Set aside in a warm place for 15 minutes or until the surface starts to foam.

Sift the flour, bicarbonate of soda, salt and vanilla into a large bowl. Add the yeast mixture and stir to combine. Place a clean damp tea towel over the mixing bowl and set aside for 35–40 minutes or until the mixture is risen and bubbly.

Preheat the oven to 100°C fan-forced.

Lightly grease a large frying pan and set over medium–high heat, then lightly grease a few egg rings and place them in the pan.

Stir the mixture again – it should look like thick, bubbly pancake batter. Add 60 ml–125 ml (¼ cup–½ cup) more water to reach the desired consistency if necessary.

Spoon 2–3 tablespoons of the mixture into each egg ring. Cook for 2 minutes or until the tops are completely covered in bubbles and the batter is dry. Remove the egg rings, transfer the crumpets to a heatproof plate and keep warm in the oven. Repeat with the remaining mixture to make about 20 crumpets.

Serve the warm crumpets with your favourite toppings. I love adding lashings of vegan butter and maple syrup!

Any leftover crumpets will keep in an airtight container in the fridge for 2–3 days or in the freezer for up to 2 weeks.

Brekkie

MACADAMIA GRANOLA

I absolutely love making my own granola. Not only is it healthier for you than store-bought granola, it's also super quick and much easier to make than you might think. This granola was inspired by my love for Aussie macadamias. These nuts remind me of my childhood – cracking them fresh after my dad brought them home from the orchards, or when my nan picked them up as a gift on her way to visit us. Macadamias are really fatty and delicious, and taste absolutely amazing when roasted.

Makes 3 cups
160 g (1 cup) macadamias
100 g (1 cup) rolled oats
3 tablespoons hemp seeds
85 g (½ cup) buckwheat kernels
pinch of sea salt
2 teaspoons ground cinnamon
3 tablespoons coconut nectar
2 tablespoons olive oil
1 teaspoon vanilla extract
25 g coconut flakes

To serve
plant-based milk
Coconut Yoghurt (see page 264)
fresh berries

Preheat the oven to 160°C fan-forced. Line a baking tray with baking paper.

Place the macadamias, oats, hemp seeds, buckwheat kernels, salt and cinnamon in a large bowl and stir to combine.

In another bowl, combine the coconut nectar, olive oil and vanilla. Pour this mixture into the dry ingredients and stir until everything is well coated.

Spread the mixture onto the prepared tray and bake for 15 minutes or until lightly golden. Remove from the oven and allow to completely cool before transferring to an airtight jar or container.

The granola will keep in the fridge for up to 3 weeks. Serve with your favourite plant-based milk or coconut yoghurt and some berries.

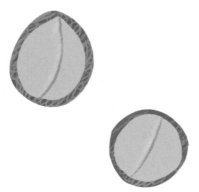

MOONSHINE MORNING
SMOOTHIE BOWL

This is my absolute favourite smoothie bowl. Thousands of visitors to Bali have tried this dish on my menu at the Peloton Supershop cafe in Berawa, and I continue to have people tagging me in photos of it! It's named the moonshine smoothie bowl because we cut the fruit into moon shapes at the cafe.

Serves 2

2 bananas, frozen
150 g frozen pink dragon fruit (see Tips)
2 teaspoons peanut butter
2 teaspoons cacao powder
½ teaspoon spirulina
60 ml–125 ml (¼ cup–½ cup) almond milk

To serve

⅓ cup Macadamia Granola (see page 29)
   or use store-bought
fresh fruit, such as dragon fruit,
   strawberries and papaya
coconut flakes
pumpkin seeds
mint leaves
edible flowers

Place the banana, dragon fruit, peanut butter, cacao powder, spirulina and 60 ml (¼ cup) of the almond milk in a blender and blend on high until smooth and creamy. If it's too thick, add the remaining almond milk (see Tips).

Divide the smoothie between two bowls and decorate with the granola, fruit, coconut flakes, pumpkin seeds, mint leaves and edible flowers.

• •

TIPS

Some supermarkets and health-food stores sell packets of frozen dragon fruit cubes. Look for them near the sachets of frozen acai and berries.

The trick to a thick and creamy smoothie bowl is to use frozen fruit and start with less liquid, only adding extra if needed.

• •

Brekkie

FLUFFY MAPLE BAKON PANCAKES

These maple bakon pancakes are the fluffiest pancakes I have ever created! The batter itself may taste a little sour from the baking powder and apple cider vinegar, but the flavours balance out once the pancakes are cooked and drizzled with maple syrup. Maple bacon pancakes appear on most US hotel breakfast and cafe menus, so when I developed my vegan bakon recipes, I thought it would be nice to include a pancake breakfast dish.

Serves 2
150 g (1 cup) plain flour
1 tablespoon baking powder
½ teaspoon sea salt
250 ml (1 cup) soy milk
1 teaspoon vanilla extract
1 tablespoon pure maple syrup,
  plus extra for drizzling
1 tablespoon apple cider vinegar
1 tablespoon coconut oil
½ × quantity Coconut Bakon (see page 289)
handful of mixed fresh berries, to serve

Sift the flour, baking powder and salt into a large mixing bowl and stir to combine. Make a well in the centre and pour in the soy milk, vanilla, maple syrup and apple cider vinegar. Stir everything together and set aside.

Preheat the oven to 120°C fan-forced.

Heat a large non-stick frying pan over high heat. Wait until fully heated, then add ½ teaspoon of the coconut oil and swirl around the pan. Add 80 ml (⅓ cup) of the pancake batter and cook for 1–2 minutes or until bubbles form across the top. Flip and cook for a further 30–45 seconds or until just cooked through. Remove from the pan and set aside on a heatproof plate in the warm oven while you cook the remaining pancakes.

Serve the pancakes topped with a drizzle of maple syrup, the coconut bakon and fresh berries.

DRIED MANGO MUESLI

Unlike most store-bought muesli, this recipe is free from processed sugar. It can also be made 100 per cent gluten free if you swap the rolled oats for gluten-free oats (oats are processed in facilities that also process gluten, so they can't be labelled as GF). The dried mango in this muesli mix is inspired by the countless packets of dried mango we devoured in the Philippines and Thailand. If you happen to visit the Philippines, get stuck into their mangoes! They're the best I have ever tasted.

Makes 1 × 1 litre jar
200 g (2 cups) rolled oats
55 g (⅓ cup) flax seeds
55 g (⅓ cup) chia seeds
55 g (⅓ cup) hemp seeds
50 g (⅓ cup) pumpkin seeds
50 g dried mango, roughly chopped
2 medjool dates, pitted and diced
60 g (1 cup) shredded coconut

Place all the ingredients in a bowl and stir to combine. Store in an airtight jar in the pantry for up to 2 months.

Serve the muesli with any plant-based milk or soak in plant-based milk overnight for a bircher muesli. It's also delicious added to smoothies or served with coconut yoghurt.

KETO BIRCHER

During my vegan keto experiment late last year, I created this low-carb bircher and became absolutely obsessed with it! It's super quick to put together, and if you make a big batch you only need to add liquid to one serving for the next day. Nutritionally, this dish is a powerhouse; it's packed with healthy fats including a great ratio of omega-3 fatty acids. It's also very low in sugar and high in fibre. Make it the night before and simply top with fruit in the morning to take with you to work – it will power you through until lunchtime.

Serves 2
2 tablespoons hemp seeds
2 tablespoons flax seeds
2 tablespoons chia seeds
3 tablespoons chopped macadamias
3 tablespoons shredded coconut
125 ml (½ cup) coconut milk
¼ teaspoon vanilla extract
4–5 drops liquid stevia

To serve
2 handfuls of mixed fresh berries
125 g (½ cup) Coconut Yoghurt (see page 264)
   or 125 ml (½ cup) coconut milk
ground cinnamon
nut butter
shredded coconut
chopped almonds
mint leaves
edible flowers

Place all the ingredients and 375 ml (1½ cups) of water in a bowl. Stir to combine, then cover and place in the fridge overnight.

The next day, spoon the bircher into two bowls and top with fresh berries, coconut yoghurt or coconut milk, cinnamon, nut butter, shredded coconut, almonds, mint leaves and edible flowers.

- - - - - - - - - - - - - - - - - - -

TIP
You can also add grated carrot to the bircher, making it a fantastic way to increase your veggie intake.

- - - - - - - - - - - - - - - - - - -

PECAN–MAPLE
BANANA BREAD

After receiving so much love for the peanut-nana bread in my first cookbook, I wanted to create and share a new nutty banana bread recipe. The crunchy maple-roasted pecans on top of this loaf give it a delicious new twist, and it tastes like a pecan pie and banana bread hybrid! This recipe is inspired by my travels to the United States where 80 per cent of the world's pecans are grown.

Serves 8
75 g (¾ cup) pecans
1 tablespoon pure maple syrup
sea salt
½ teaspoon olive oil
3 large ripe bananas
1 teaspoon vanilla extract
1 tablespoon chia seeds
3 tablespoons vegan butter
110 g (½ cup) coconut sugar
250 ml (1 cup) soy milk
120 g (1 cup) spelt flour
150 g (1 cup) plain flour
3 teaspoons baking powder
1 teaspoon ground cinnamon

To serve
vegan butter, nut butter or pure maple syrup

Preheat the oven to 150°C fan-forced. Line a baking tray and a 20 cm × 10 cm loaf tin with baking paper.

Combine the pecans, maple syrup, a pinch of salt and the olive oil in a bowl and massage together with your hands. Transfer to the prepared baking tray and bake for 10–15 minutes or until the pecans are caramelised. Set aside to cool and increase the oven temperature to 180°C.

Mash the bananas in a bowl and stir through the vanilla extract and chia seeds. Set aside.

Place the vegan butter and coconut sugar in a large mixing bowl and use a hand-held mixer to beat until smooth and fluffy. Add the soy milk and mashed banana and mix well to combine.

Sift the flours, baking powder, cinnamon and a pinch of salt into a separate bowl.

Pour the wet mixture into the dry ingredients and gently fold together until just mixed. Pour the batter into the prepared loaf tin and top with the caramelised pecans.

Bake for 50–60 minutes or until a skewer inserted into the centre of the bread comes out clean. Allow the bread to cool for 15 minutes, then turn out onto a wire rack to cool for a further 10 minutes.

Slice and eat warm with a smear of vegan butter, nut butter or maple syrup.

BEAUTY SMOOTHIE BOWL

This smoothie bowl is high in antioxidants from the bright berries and beetroot powder. I've also added hemp seeds for their omega-3 profile. I was inspired to make this dish after our trip to Finland, where we learned about local wild fruits that grow in their winter climate.

Serves 1

1 banana, frozen
60 g (½ cup) frozen raspberries
3 strawberries, frozen
1 teaspoon beetroot powder (see Tip)
¼ teaspoon vanilla powder
2 teaspoons cashew butter
125 ml (½ cup) Vanilla Hemp and Maca Milk
  (see page 262)

To serve

⅓ cup Macadamia Granola (see page 29)
  or use store-bought
1 tablespoon hemp seeds
1 tablespoon cashew butter
½ banana, sliced
handful of mixed fresh berries
dried edible flowers

• • • • • • • • • • • • • • • • • •

TIP

You can find beetroot powder at most health-food stores and some chemists.

• • • • • • • • • • • • • • • • • •

Place all the ingredients in a blender and blend until smooth.

Transfer to a bowl and decorate the smoothie with the granola, hemp seeds, cashew butter, banana, fresh berries and edible flowers.

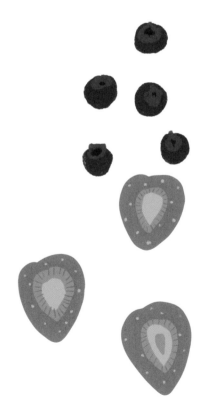

VEGAN FRIED EGGS

These vegan fried eggs went viral on my YouTube channel last year and I'm so excited to share the recipe with you! I came up with the idea while trying to recreate banh xeo (see page 154) after my travels to Vietnam. Those crispy rice pancakes gave me the idea of how to create an egg white, while my cheeze sauce recipe (see page 280) inspired the yolk. I have created three vegan egg dishes for you to try (see page 46 for scrambled eggs or page 49 for an omelette). The key ingredient in all of them is kala namak (Himalayan black salt), which has an eggy odour and taste.

Serves 4
olive oil, for frying
toasted sourdough slices, to serve
smashed avocado, to serve
chilli salt, to serve
freshly ground black pepper, to serve

Egg yolk
170 g peeled and deseeded pumpkin
1 tablespoon nutritional yeast flakes
¼ teaspoon kala namak (Himalayan black salt) (see Tip)
¼ teaspoon freshly ground black pepper
pinch of sea salt
2 tablespoons olive oil
2 tablespoons cornflour

Egg white
3 tablespoons rice flour
3 tablespoons coconut milk
pinch of sea salt

· · · · · · · · · · · · · · · · · · · ·

TIP
Kala namak can be purchased from some health-food stores and online.

· · · · · · · · · · · · · · · · · · · ·

Preheat the oven to 120°C fan-forced.

To make the egg yolk, bring a saucepan of water to the boil, add the pumpkin and boil until soft. Drain well, then transfer to the bowl of a food processor or blender. Add the remaining egg yolk ingredients and 2 tablespoons of water. Process or blend until smooth – the mixture should be thick but still runny enough to drip off a spoon.

Whisk the egg white ingredients and 1 tablespoon of water in a bowl.

Heat a drizzle of oil in a large frying pan over medium–high heat. Spoon 2 tablespoons of the egg white mixture into the pan, then cover and cook for 10 seconds. Remove the lid and carefully spoon 1 tablespoon of the yolk mixture into the centre of the white. Replace the lid for another 30 seconds or until the white starts to crisp around the edge. Transfer to a heatproof plate and place in the oven to keep warm. Repeat with the remaining ingredients – you should have enough to make about eight eggs.

Serve the eggs on toast with smashed avocado, chilli salt and pepper. Leftover mixture will keep in airtight containers in the fridge for up to 3 days.

VEGAN SCRAMBLED EGGS

This is definitely the easiest of my vegan egg recipes as it's essentially a tofu scramble. It is one of my favourite protein-packed post-gym breakfasts, as it's quick to make and provides about 8 grams of protein per serve. I usually cook with firm tofu, but I've come to realise that soft or medium tofu is best for scrambling, because it has more liquid.

Serves 2
200 g soft or medium tofu
1 tablespoon nutritional yeast flakes
1 teaspoon olive oil
pinch of freshly ground black pepper
pinch of sea salt
pinch of kala namak (Himalayan black salt) (see Tip)
pinch of ground turmeric
2 garlic cloves, crushed

To serve
toasted sourdough slices
sliced avocado
chilli flakes
dill fronds
micro herbs (optional)

Place all the ingredients in a bowl and lightly mash, keeping the tofu quite chunky.

Heat a non-stick frying pan over medium–high heat and add the tofu mixture.

Sauté for 2–3 minutes or until starting to turn golden. If liquid starts to leach from the tofu, cover the pan with a lid and drain most of the liquid away. Return the pan to the heat and fry for a further 1–2 minutes or until golden.

Serve on sourdough toast with sliced avocado, a few chilli flakes, dill fronds and micro herbs (if using).

TIP
Kala namak can be purchased from some health-food stores and online.

MUSHROOM & TOMATO OMELETTE

I have been making vegan fried eggs and scrambled eggs for some time, but it was only when I had perfected these that I thought about making a vegan omelette. So, here it is! I have added tofu for an extra protein punch, along with kala namak (Himalayan black salt) for that eggy flavour.

Serves 1
25 g rice flour or besan (chickpea flour)
100 g medium tofu
1½ tablespoons soy milk
1 tablespoon nutritional yeast flakes
pinch of ground turmeric
pinch of freshly ground black pepper
pinch of sea salt
pinch of kala namak (Himalayan black salt) (see Tips)
1 teaspoon olive oil
1 button mushroom, sliced
4 cherry tomatoes, halved
handful of baby spinach leaves

To serve
chilli flakes
snow pea sprouts
olive oil
toasted sourdough slices (optional)
lemon wedges (optional)

Place the rice flour or besan, tofu, soy milk, nutritional yeast, spices and salts in a blender and blend until smooth.

Heat the oil in a small non-stick frying pan over medium–high heat and pour the omelette mixture into the pan. Add the mushroom, tomato and spinach and fry the omelette for 3 minutes or until the bottom is golden and cooked through. Gently fold the omelette in half and continue to cook for a further minute (see Tips).

Top with chilli flakes, snow pea sprouts and a drizzle of olive oil and serve with sourdough toast and lemon wedges for squeezing over, if you like.

- - - - - - - - - - - - - - - - - - - -

TIPS

Make sure your omelette is completely cooked through before attempting to fold it in half. If your omelette doesn't hold its shape, don't worry – it will still taste absolutely delicious!

Kala namak can be purchased from some health-food stores and online.

- - - - - - - - - - - - - - - - - - - -

MEXICAN MOLLETES

This was my favourite breakfast in Mexico. Molletes are open toasted sandwiches most commonly served with stewed black beans and guacamole. They are like a Mexican version of baked beans on toast! Beans are such a fabulous plant-based breakfast option, as they're packed with protein and fibre. Black beans are also a good source of iron.

Serves 2

400 g can black beans, top quarter of
  liquid drained
sea salt
½ teaspoon ground cumin
125 ml (½ cup) vegetable stock
1 avocado
½ teaspoon freshly ground black pepper
4 slices sourdough, toasted

To serve
snow pea sprouts
pickled red onion (see page 286)
chilli powder

Place the black beans and their liquid, ½ teaspoon of salt, the cumin and stock in a saucepan over medium heat. Simmer for 20–25 minutes or until the liquid is absorbed and the mixture begins to thicken.

In a bowl, mash the avocado with the pepper and a pinch of salt.

Spread the mashed avocado on the toast and top with the beans, sprouts and pickled onion. Finish with a pinch of chilli powder.

HASH BROWNS

WITH TURMERIC–CASHEW SAUCE

This tasty breakfast is another dish inspired by my time living in Bali. I used to visit a cafe named Quince, where they made the best hash browns, and I decided to try making my own version. I love the combination of hash brown, sweet pumpkin and creamy cashew sauce, all piled high with herbs.

Serves 2
350 g potatoes
2 tablespoons plain flour
2 tablespoons finely chopped rosemary
1 tablespoon finely snipped chives
¼ teaspoon sea salt
1 tablespoon avocado oil

Pumpkin and chickpea topping
150 g peeled and deseeded pumpkin,
   cut into 1 cm cubes
80 g (½ cup) drained and rinsed canned chickpeas
2 teaspoons pure maple syrup
2 teaspoons olive oil
pinch of sea salt

Turmeric–cashew sauce
50 g (⅓ cup) cashews, preferably soaked in
   cold water overnight and drained
¼ teaspoon ground turmeric
1½ tablespoons freshly squeezed lemon juice,
   plus lemon wedges to serve
¼ teaspoon sea salt
1 teaspoon olive oil
1 teaspoon apple cider vinegar
pinch of freshly ground black pepper

To serve
½ avocado, sliced
handful of dill fronds
handful of micro herbs
1 tablespoon hemp seeds

Preheat the oven to 180°C fan-forced.

Combine the ingredients for the pumpkin and chickpea topping in a baking dish and bake for 35 minutes or until golden and crisp. Set aside.

Meanwhile, grate the potatoes into a colander. Rinse with water, then squeeze out as much liquid as possible. Transfer to a plate lined with paper towel or a clean tea towel to completely dry.

To make the turmeric–cashew sauce, place all the ingredients and 3 tablespoons of water in a blender and blend until smooth. Check the seasoning and add more salt, if desired. Set aside.

Transfer the potato to a large bowl and stir through the flour, herbs and salt.

Heat the oil in a large frying pan over high heat and spoon in ⅓ cup of the potato mixture to make each hash brown – you should get four in total. Spread each one out to form a 1 cm-thick circle. (Alternatively use egg rings.) Fry on each side for 2–3 minutes or until golden and crisp, then transfer to a plate lined with paper towel to soak up excess oil.

Place a hash brown on each plate and top with the pumpkin and chickpea mixture. Position the remaining hash browns on top and spoon the turmeric–cashew sauce around the plate. Serve with the sliced avocado and lemon wedges on the side and top everything with the herbs, hemp seeds and a little extra salt and pepper.

NOURISHING POWER BOWL

This savoury breakfast bowl with quinoa, protein-rich vegan scrambled eggs, satisfying fats from avocado, tahini and hemp and a punch of vitamins and minerals from pumpkin and kale is hearty enough to power you through an active morning. This recipe draws inspiration from a few different places, but especially from one of my favourite breakfast spots on the Gold Coast, Stable Coffee Kitchen in Currumbin.

Serves 2

450 g peeled and deseeded pumpkin,
   cut into two 5 cm thick wedges
2 teaspoons olive oil
pinch of ground cinnamon
pinch of sea salt
65 g (⅓ cup) tri-colour quinoa
80 g (2 cups) shredded kale leaves
1 × quantity Vegan Scrambled Eggs (see page 46)
1 avocado, halved, stone removed
handful of snow pea sprouts
4 cubes of Marinated Almond–Macadamia Feta
   (see page 270)
1 tablespoon hemp seeds
pinch of chilli flakes
2 lemon cheeks

Sweet tahini sauce

2 tablespoons tahini
2 teaspoons tamari or soy sauce
2 teaspoons pure maple syrup

Preheat the oven to 180°C fan-forced. Line a baking tray with baking paper.

Place the pumpkin on the prepared tray, brush with half the oil and sprinkle over the cinnamon and salt. Bake for 40–45 minutes or until soft and golden.

Meanwhile, make the sweet tahini sauce by whisking the ingredients and 1 tablespoon of water in a bowl. Set aside.

Bring 375 ml (1½ cups) of water to the boil in a saucepan over high heat. Add the quinoa, then reduce the heat to medium, cover and simmer for 8–12 minutes or until the water has evaporated and the quinoa is cooked through and fluffy.

Meanwhile, heat the remaining oil in a frying pan over medium–high heat, add the kale and sauté for 4–5 minutes or until wilted and dark green. Transfer to serving bowls, along with the quinoa and vegan scrambled eggs.

Smear the sauce along one side of the serving bowls, then place your cooked pumpkin on top. Add the avocado halves and top with the snow pea sprouts, feta, hemp seeds and chilli flakes. Serve with the lemon cheeks.

BREAKFAST TACOS

These little beauties are inspired by our visit to Mexico where I became devoted to all things taco! Typically, a breakfast taco contains scrambled egg, so I thought here is the perfect opportunity to use my delicious vegan scrambled egg recipe.

Serves 2
6 mini corn tortillas
1 avocado
juice of ½ lime
pinch of sea salt
½ sweetcorn cob, kernels removed
1 × quantity Vegan Scrambled Eggs (see page 46)
6 cherry tomatoes, halved or quartered
3 tablespoons canned black beans,
 drained and rinsed

To serve
½ fresh jalapeño, finely sliced
coriander leaves
snow pea sprouts
pickled red onion (see page 286)
lime wedges

Heat a frying pan over medium heat and, working in batches, pan-fry the tortillas for 10 seconds on each side. Wrap in a clean tea towel to keep warm.

In a bowl, mash the avocado with the lime juice and salt.

In the same frying pan over medium heat, fry the sweetcorn for 2 minutes or until lightly golden.

Spoon a heaped tablespoon of vegan scrambled egg onto each tortilla. Top with 1 tablespoon of smashed avocado, a cherry tomato and 2 teaspoons each of sweetcorn and black beans. Finish with a slice of jalapeño, coriander leaves, snow pea sprouts and pickled red onion. Serve with lime wedges.

SMASHED AVO & FETA ON TOAST

My favourite breakfast is and always will be good old avocado on toast. I've added my new almond–macadamia feta to this recipe, as I wanted to show how you can elevate this simple breakfast to another level.

Serves 2
1 large avocado
2 tablespoons freshly squeezed lemon juice
sea salt and freshly ground black pepper
1 teaspoon extra-virgin olive oil
3 tablespoons Marinated Almond–Macadamia Feta
  (see page 270)
4 slices sourdough, toasted
chilli flakes, to serve (optional)

. . . .

TIP
If you'd like to make this a more filling brekkie, try adding a serve of vegan scrambled eggs (see page 46) on top.

. . . .

Place the avocado, lemon juice, salt, pepper and olive oil in a bowl. Mash together, keeping it moderately chunky (none of that pureed avo here!) and fold through the feta.

Scoop the smashed avo and feta onto your toast and sprinkle with extra salt and pepper, and chilli flakes, if desired.

VEGAN TOASTIE

When it comes to handy on-the-go brekkies, a good toastie is unbeatable. I love the combination of baked pumpkin and creamy hot avocado sandwiched between two pieces of deliciously crunchy sourdough bread. The pesto also gives this toastie a big flavour hit.

Serves 2

4 × 1 cm thick slices peeled and deseeded pumpkin
3 teaspoons olive oil, plus extra for brushing
½ avocado
juice of ½ lemon
sea salt and freshly ground black pepper
40 g (1 cup) shredded kale leaves
4 slices sourdough
2 tablespoons pesto
½ tomato, sliced
3–4 tablespoons Vegan Mozzarella (see page 267)
  or use store-bought
½ teaspoon chilli flakes

Preheat the oven to 180°C fan-forced.

Place the pumpkin on a baking tray, drizzle over 2 teaspoons of the oil and bake for 25–30 minutes or until soft and cooked through. Transfer to a bowl and lightly mash with the back of a fork.

In a bowl, mash the avocado with the lemon juice and season with salt and pepper.

Heat the remaining oil in a small frying pan over medium heat. Add the kale and sauté for 1 minute or until just wilted.

Preheat a sandwich press.

Brush the sourdough slices on one side with a little olive oil. Spread the pesto on the other side of two slices and top with the sautéed kale, pumpkin, tomato, avocado and vegan mozzarella. Sandwich together with the remaining bread, with the oiled side facing upwards. Transfer the toasties to the sandwich press and toast for 3 minutes or until golden and crispy. Alternatively, place the toasties on a baking tray and toast in the oven for 10–15 minutes.

Cut the toasties in half, sprinkle with the chilli flakes and a little salt and serve.

LIGHT | MEALS

BUFFALO CAULIFLOWER WINGS

This dish is inspired by my travels in the United States, where buffalo wings are a popular snack. Throughout NYC and LA, I noticed a trend for replacing the chicken with cauliflower and it was totally delicious! The spicy glaze was enough to make you keep coming back for more, and the cool ranch dipping sauce perfectly balanced out the spice. I have baked the cauliflower instead of frying it, but this does make the final result less crispy. If you would prefer something more like the original, you can shallow-fry the cauliflower for 3–4 minutes, until golden and crisp all over. Just remember to drain the florets on paper towel to soak up excess oil, and never re-use your oil as reheating it changes its chemical structure, creating trans-fats.

Serves 2–4
1 head (approximately 600 g) cauliflower, broken into florets
finely chopped flat-leaf parsley leaves, to serve
Ranch Dipping Sauce (see page 278), to serve

Batter
75 g (½ cup) plain flour
½ teaspoon baking powder
2 teaspoons smoked paprika
1 teaspoon garlic powder
½ teaspoon sea salt
½ teaspoon freshly ground black pepper
125 ml (½ cup) soy milk

Spicy marinade
1 tablespoon sriracha chilli sauce or hot sauce
2 teaspoons olive oil
2 teaspoons pure maple syrup
1 teaspoon tamari or soy sauce

Preheat the oven to 180°C fan-forced. Line a large baking tray with baking paper.

To make the batter, sift the flour, baking powder, spices and salt into a large mixing bowl. Add the pepper, soy milk and 1–2 tablespoons of water and whisk to form a smooth, thick batter.

Add the cauliflower florets to the batter and mix well, ensuring each piece is evenly coated.

Transfer to the baking tray in a single layer, preferably with a little space between each floret, and bake for 20 minutes.

Meanwhile, combine the spicy marinade ingredients in a bowl.

Remove the tray from the oven and brush the marinade all over the cauliflower, then return to the oven and bake for a further 20 minutes or until golden.

Transfer the cauliflower to a serving plate, scatter over some chopped parsley and serve immediately with the ranch sauce for dipping.

'SOM TAM'

Here is my version of a green papaya salad or 'som tam' for when you can't find green papaya! I know from a few attempts at making this salad that green papaya can be hard to find in Australia, so I decided to give this traditional Thai dish an accessible twist using zucchini, carrot and red cabbage. It's great as a light lunch or side salad.

Serves 2

150 g zucchini, julienned
1 carrot, julienned
75 g (1 cup) finely shredded red cabbage
6 snow peas, julienned
1½ tablespoons tamari or soy sauce
2 garlic cloves
2 long red chillies (or use bird's eye chillies
  if you like it spicy), roughly chopped
1 tablespoon freshly squeezed lime juice
1 teaspoon coconut sugar
1 teaspoon Vegan Fish Sauce (see page 275)
  (optional)
¼ teaspoon sea salt
10 cherry tomatoes
3 tablespoons unsalted peanuts, roughly chopped

Combine the zucchini, carrot, cabbage and snow peas in a large bowl.

Using a large mortar and pestle, pound the garlic, chilli, lime juice, coconut sugar, vegan fish sauce (if using) and salt to form a paste. Add the cherry tomatoes and gently pound in the paste to soften.

Spoon the tomatoes and paste over the salad and toss to combine. Sprinkle over the chopped peanuts and serve.

Light meals

TASMANIAN
HEMP & PUMPKIN SALAD

When we were in Tasmania, we visited a hemp farm right before harvest. We were lucky enough to have dinner in the field, surrounded by great people, while learning so much about this amazing plant. Our friends made this beautiful salad for us while we were there and we've been making it ever since.

Serves 3–4

400 g pumpkin, skin on, deseeded and
   cut into 2 cm cubes (see Tip)
2 teaspoons olive oil
pinch of sea salt
pinch of ground cinnamon
120 g (3 cups) roughly shredded kale leaves
50 g (½ cup) diced broccoli
2 tablespoons freshly squeezed lemon juice
150 g tempeh, cut into 2 cm × 5 mm pieces
2 tablespoons coconut aminos
2 tablespoons hemp seeds
35 g (⅓ cup) walnuts, roughly chopped
1 tomato, diced
1 avocado, diced
handful of pea shoots, trimmed
freshly ground black pepper

· · · · · · · · · · · · · · · · · · ·

TIP
*Keep the seeds from the pumpkin to
make my crispy pumpkin seeds on
page 265.*

· · · · · · · · · · · · · · · · · · ·

Preheat the oven to 180°C fan-forced.

Place the pumpkin in a baking dish and toss through half the oil, along with the sea salt and cinnamon. Transfer to the oven and bake for 30 minutes or until golden and cooked through. Allow the pumpkin to cool for 5–10 minutes, then gently squash with the back of a fork.

Meanwhile, place the kale, broccoli and lemon juice in a salad bowl and toss to combine. Set aside.

Heat the remaining oil in a frying pan over medium heat and fry the tempeh for 3 minutes, tossing regularly, until golden and crispy. Transfer to a bowl, pour over the coconut aminos and toss to coat. Set aside.

Add the hemp seeds, walnuts, tomato and avocado to the kale and broccoli and toss everything together. Add the pumpkin and tempeh to the salad and mix well to combine. Transfer to a serving bowl, scatter over the pea shoots, season with pepper and serve.

Light meals

PULLED JACKFRUIT
DUMPLINGS

The dumplings in my first cookbook were really popular, so after I returned from my travels in South East Asia I decided to create an equally delicious dumpling recipe for this book, combining inspiration from South Korean dumplings (mandu) and Vietnamese dumplings (banh cuon). Here, I've used jackfruit to give a pulled pork–like texture and added a spicy and salty sauce so that each bite keeps you coming back for more!

Makes 20

1 tablespoon olive oil, plus extra for frying
   the dumplings (optional)
1 onion, finely diced
2 garlic cloves, crushed
1 teaspoon five spice powder
400 g can young jackfruit, drained and rinsed,
   roughly chopped
¼ red capsicum, finely diced
250 ml (1 cup) vegetable stock
250 g packet round dumpling wrappers
   (see Tip, overleaf)

Chilli–soy sauce

2 tablespoons sriracha chilli sauce
2 tablespoons tamari or soy sauce
2 tablespoons Vegan Fish Sauce (see page 275)
1 tablespoon coconut sugar

Accompaniments (optional)

2 tablespoons crispy fried shallots
1 spring onion, finely sliced
Sriracha Mayo (see page 282) or sriracha chilli sauce
handful of coriander or sorrel leaves
1 teaspoon sesame seeds
tamari or soy sauce, for dipping

Whisk the chilli–soy sauce ingredients in a bowl and set aside.

Heat the oil in a frying pan over medium heat and add the onion, garlic and five spice powder. Fry for 1 minute, then add the jackfruit and capsicum, along with the vegetable stock.

Simmer for 10 minutes or until the liquid has reduced, then gently mash the jackfruit using the back of a fork to break up some of the larger chunks. Reduce the heat to medium–low, pour in the sauce and stir to combine, then simmer for a further 2–3 minutes. Remove from the heat and set the mixture aside to cool.

Once the mixture is cool enough to handle, you can begin to make your dumplings. There are many different ways to fold dumplings and it doesn't really matter which way you choose, as they will all taste the same. I find the easiest way is to hold a dumpling wrapper in the palm of your hand and place 2 teaspoons of the mixture in the centre. Fold the wrapper in half to make a semi-circle, then crimp the edge with a fork to seal. Place on a tray lined with baking paper, then repeat with the remaining filling and wrappers to make about 20 dumplings, keeping the dumplings evenly spaced apart so they don't stick together.

RECIPE CONTINUED OVER THE PAGE ▶

To steam the dumplings, working in batches, place the dumplings in a lined steamer set over a saucepan of simmering water. Steam for 2–3 minutes or until translucent and moist.

To fry the dumplings, heat a little oil in a non-stick frying pan and, working in batches, add the dumplings so they are evenly spaced apart. Fry, covered, for 2–3 minutes on one side or until they look steamed and cooked through. Turn the dumplings over and fry the other side, if you like.

Serve with any or all of the accompaniments.

If you have any leftover filling, store it in the fridge for up to 3 days and serve with any salad or Buddha bowl.

TIP

You can find dumpling wrappers in the frozen section of some supermarkets, but Asian supermarkets will always have them. They are usually vegan, but check the ingredients as some brands use egg.

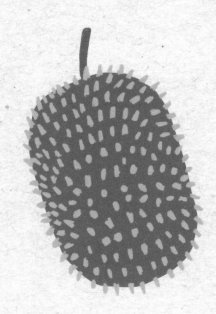

RICE PAPER ROLLS

Vietnamese rice paper rolls make a fresh and healthy snack or lunch. They can be packed for school or work, but I love them most when they're just freshly rolled. During a recent trip to Vietnam, we learned that the key to an authentic rice paper roll is to keep it really simple and use plenty of fresh herbs.

Serves 2

2 teaspoons avocado oil
100 g medium tofu, cut into
  thin strips
70 g oyster mushrooms, torn
¼ teaspoon five spice powder
8–10 rice paper sheets
1 small cos lettuce, leaves
  separated
2 cups mixed herbs, such as
  Vietnamese mint,
  Thai basil and coriander
1 Lebanese cucumber, cut into
  long batons
10 sticks pickled daikon or carrot
  (see page 286)
1 long red chilli, finely sliced
  (optional)
1 avocado, sliced

To serve

3 tablespoons Nuoc Cham
  (see page 278)
3 tablespoons roasted unsalted
  peanuts, roughly chopped

Heat the oil in a frying pan over medium–high heat. Add the tofu and mushroom to the pan and fry for 1 minute on each side or until golden. Sprinkle over the five spice and transfer to a small bowl.

Lay out all the remaining ingredients in front of you.

Using a clean damp tea towel, lightly wet a rice paper sheet on both sides and place it on a clean work surface. Add a little of each ingredient along the centre of the rice paper, then fold both ends into the centre and place a pair of chopsticks over the filling to keep it in place. Starting with the end closest to you, gently lift the rice paper sheet over the filling and chopsticks and roll away from you until you have a tight rice paper roll. Gently pull the chopsticks out and repeat with the remaining rice paper sheets and filling.

To serve, divide the nuoc cham among dipping bowls and sprinkle over the peanuts.

• •

TIPS

In Vietnam, I learned that rice paper sheets are only lightly moistened by rubbing a damp cloth over each side. This makes the rice paper chewier and slightly crunchy, which I absolutely love.

You'll quickly learn how much filling to put in your rice paper rolls, as overfilling will lead to your roll exploding! I usually find my groove by the third roll.

You may like to only fold in one end of your rice paper rolls, leaving the herbs and veggies sprouting out the top. I prefer to make mine this way, as it allows me to pour the dipping sauce into the roll and munch away.

CHIPOTLE & CAPSICUM
HUMMUS WITH CRUDITES

I absolutely love this hummus recipe! The chipotle sauce gives it a delicious spicy and smoky flavour and takes traditional hummus in a completely different direction.

Makes 1½ cups
1 red capsicum, cut into 2 cm wide strips
400 g can chickpeas, drained and rinsed (see Tip)
1 tablespoon olive oil, plus extra to serve
1½ tablespoons chipotle sauce
2 garlic cloves
1 teaspoon ground cumin
½ teaspoon chilli powder, plus extra to serve
3 tablespoons freshly squeezed lemon juice
½ teaspoon sea salt
micro herbs, to garnish (optional)
sliced sourdough, to serve

Crudites suggestions
carrot sticks
halved radishes
cucumber batons
sliced red capsicum
cauliflower florets

• • • • • • • • • • • • • • • • • •

TIP
Keep your chickpea liquid (aquafaba) to make the sriracha mayo on page 282.

• • • • • • • • • • • • • • • • • •

Preheat the oven to 180°C fan-forced. Line a baking tray with baking paper.

Place the capsicum on the prepared tray and bake for 25 minutes. Set a few chickpeas aside for garnish.

Place the remaining chickpeas, the olive oil, chipotle sauce, garlic, spices, lemon juice and salt in a blender and add three-quarters of the cooked capsicum. Blend until smooth.

Transfer the hummus to a bowl, then dice the remaining capsicum and scatter over the top along with the reserved chickpeas and micro herbs (if using). Drizzle over a little extra olive oil and a sprinkling of chilli powder, and serve with sliced sourdough and your choice of crudites on a beautiful share platter.

TOM KHA GAI
WITH MUSHROOMS

Tom kha gai is my favourite Thai soup, as it's absolutely bursting with zesty flavour. I learned how to make it during a cooking class in northern Thailand, where we picked all the fresh herbs from the garden and visited the local market to buy the veggies. This soup would make a great entree or light main on a cold winter's night.

Serves 2
250 ml (1 cup) coconut milk
3 cm piece of galangal, sliced
1 lemongrass stalk, white part only, bruised with
  the flat edge of a knife
45 g oyster mushrooms, roughly torn
100 g soft tofu, cut into 2 cm cubes
1 tomato, quartered
1 tablespoon Vegan Fish Sauce (see page 275)
  or soy sauce
1 teaspoon coconut sugar
1 long red chilli, sliced
4 kaffir lime leaves
1 tablespoon freshly squeezed lime juice
handful of coriander leaves

Place the coconut milk, galangal and lemongrass in a saucepan and bring to the boil over medium–high heat. Boil for 1 minute, then add the mushroom, tofu, tomato, vegan fish sauce or soy sauce, coconut sugar, chilli and 125 ml (½ cup) of water. Simmer for 5 minutes, add the kaffir lime leaves and simmer for another minute.

Remove from the heat and stir through the lime juice. Divide among bowls, scatter over a few coriander leaves and serve.

MORNING GLORY
WITH GARLIC & CHILLI

Morning glory is a popular dish served throughout South East Asia. I learned how to make it in Vietnam, where we picked the leaves from a local organic farm – it was so fresh and vibrant! Morning glory, also known as water spinach, has been consumed in Vietnam for many years and they believe the dark, leafy green is good for their health. I can't deny that dark leafy greens are nutritious vegetables and this dish is an excellent and quick way to pump up your greens intake. Morning glory can be difficult to find – try your local Asian grocer or farmers' market; otherwise you can use kale. It will be just as delicious.

Serves 2

4 garlic cloves, finely sliced
½ long red chilli, finely sliced
2 tablespoons Vegan Fish Sauce (see page 275)
¼ teaspoon sea salt
1 teaspoon coconut sugar
2 teaspoons freshly squeezed lime juice
1 teaspoon olive oil
200 g morning glory (water spinach)

Combine the garlic, chilli, fish sauce, salt, sugar and lime juice in a bowl.

Heat the oil in a frying pan over medium heat, add the morning glory and sauté for 1 minute or until just wilted. Pour the sauce into the pan and quickly stir-fry for a further minute.

Serve as a side dish or with my stir-fried lemongrass tofu (see page 140) and rice for an extra punch of greens!

MUSHROOM
QUESADILLAS

A quesadilla is like a taco crossed with a toastie, and what a delicious little invention it is! While in Tulum, Mexico, I ate a vegan quesadilla at a restaurant called Sanara, where they made their own coconut tortillas and vegan mozzarella. Don't be afraid to mix up this recipe and add any filling you like – roasted pumpkin and black beans would be delicious, too.

Serves 2–4
3 tablespoons vegetable stock
1 large flat mushroom, finely sliced
½ teaspoon onion powder
1 avocado
juice of ½ lime
pinch of sea salt and freshly ground black pepper
1 × quantity Vegan Mozzarella (see page 267)
8 corn tortillas
3 tablespoons Cashew Cream Cheese (see page 282)
1 fresh jalapeño, finely sliced, plus extra to serve
2 teaspoons olive oil
pickled red onion (see page 286), to serve
coriander leaves, to serve

Heat the vegetable stock and mushroom in a small saucepan over high heat. Cook, stirring frequently, until the stock has evaporated and the mushroom is golden. Sprinkle over the onion powder and set aside.

In a bowl, mash the avocado with the lime juice and salt and pepper.

Preheat a sandwich press.

Spread the vegan mozzarella onto four tortillas and top with the mushroom, a teaspoon of cashew cream and a couple of jalapeño slices. Sandwich the ingredients with the remaining tortillas and drizzle the olive oil over the top. Transfer your quesadillas to the sandwich press and cook for 2–3 minutes or until golden.

Cut the quesadillas in half and serve with the mashed avocado, remaining cashew cream cheese, pickled red onion and extra jalapeño. Top with a few coriander leaves and dig in.

SALT & PEPPER
KALAMARI

The konjac plant is mostly cultivated in South East Asia and you will typically find it at Asian supermarkets. It is very high in fibre and low in calories and you will often see it sold as low-calorie konjac noodles in supermarkets. The noodles have a chewy, gelatinous texture, which makes them a great substitute for squid.

Serves 2

160 g thick konjac noodles, cut into 3 cm lengths
45 g tapioca flour
3½ tablespoons soy milk or water
¾ teaspoon sea salt
1 teaspoon freshly ground black pepper
½ teaspoon onion powder
60 g (1 cup) panko breadcrumbs
1–4 tablespoons avocado oil
1 teaspoon chilli flakes
35 g (1 cup) rocket
large handful of snow pea sprouts
125 ml (½ cup) Sriracha Mayo (see page 282)
lemon wedges, to serve

You can bake or pan-fry the konjac kalamari. If baking, preheat the oven to 200°C fan-forced and line a baking tray with baking paper.

Place the konjac noodles in a bowl. In a separate bowl, mix the tapioca flour, soy milk or water, salt, pepper and onion powder. Place the breadcrumbs in a third bowl.

Add the konjac noodles to the bowl with the tapioca flour mixture and toss through until well coated. Transfer to the breadcrumb bowl and toss to evenly coat the noodles.

If you are baking the kalamari, transfer the noodles to the prepared tray and drizzle over 1–2 tablespoons of oil. Bake for 25 minutes or until golden and crunchy.

If you are frying the kalamari, heat 2 tablespoons of oil in a frying pan or wok. Add half the kalamari and pan-fry for 4 minutes or until golden on all sides. Transfer to a plate lined with paper towel, then add the remaining 2 tablespoons of oil to the pan and repeat with the remaining kalamari.

Sprinkle the chilli flakes over the kalamari and serve with the rocket, snow pea sprouts, sriracha mayo and lemon wedges on the side.

Light meals

SPICY MANGO & GRILLED AVOCADO SALAD

The inspiration for this light, fresh and tangy salad came from a grilled avocado dish I ate in Tulum, Mexico. I have also included some chilli mango for an extra Mexican twist!

Serves 2
1 firm mango, cut into 2 cm chunks
pinch of chilli powder
2 teaspoons freshly squeezed lime juice
1 teaspoon olive oil
1 avocado, halved, stone removed
100 g tempeh, cut into 5 mm wide strips
225 g shredded cos lettuce
handful of coriander leaves
100 g cherry tomatoes, halved
micro herbs, to garnish (optional)

Coconut–lime dressing
1 tablespoon freshly squeezed lime juice
1 tablespoon coconut aminos

To make the dressing, whisk the lime juice and coconut aminos in a small bowl. Set aside.

Place the mango in a bowl, sprinkle over the chilli powder and lime juice and set aside.

Heat the oil in a chargrill pan over high heat and place the avocado halves, flesh-side down, in the pan. Grill for 1 minute or until char lines appear, then remove the avocado and set aside.

Place the tempeh in the pan, reduce the heat to medium and fry for 1 minute on each side or until golden.

Divide the lettuce and coriander between two bowls and top with the tempeh, avocado, mango and tomato. Drizzle over the dressing, garnish with a few micro herbs (if using) and serve.

HEMP & SESAME
POPCORN TOFU

These little bites are perfect for movie nights in or entertaining guests. This recipe is inspired by our trip to Tasmania where we learned all about the hemp plant and ate hemp-crusted tempeh bites, and from my time in Bali where a local cafe made a delicious salt and pepper popcorn tofu dish.

Serves 2
3 tablespoons hemp seeds
3 tablespoons sesame seeds
200 g firm tofu, cut into 2 cm × 1 cm chunks

Rice batter
3 tablespoons rice flour
3 tablespoons coconut milk
½ teaspoon sea salt
½ teaspoon freshly ground black pepper

To serve
1 teaspoon sriracha chilli sauce
Sriracha Mayo (see page 282)
1 avocado, mashed with 1 tablespoon freshly squeezed lime juice and a pinch of sea salt and freshly ground black pepper
sorrel leaves

Preheat the oven to 180°C fan-forced. Line a baking tray with baking paper.

Combine the rice batter ingredients in a bowl. Set aside.

In a separate bowl, combine the hemp and sesame seeds.

Dunk the pieces of tofu in the rice batter, one at a time, and allow the excess batter to drip off before tossing in the seeds until evenly coated (you may like to hold the tofu with chopsticks to prevent the seeds sticking to your fingers). Transfer to the prepared tray and repeat with the remaining tofu.

Bake the tofu for 20 minutes or until golden, then transfer to a serving plate.

Using a toothpick, swirl the sriracha chilli sauce through the sriracha mayo.

Serve the tofu bites with the mashed avocado, sriracha mayo and a few sorrel leaves scattered over the top.

Light meals

BROWN RICE
&
BAKED TOFU SALAD

When I lived in Bali, this warm salad was one of my favourite dishes. It is simple to make and contains a great balance of carbs, fats and protein. I love topping my salads with hemp seeds, as they add even more nutrition.

Serves 2
250 g firm tofu, cut into 2 cm cubes
¼ teaspoon sea salt
½ teaspoon freshly ground black pepper
2 teaspoons sesame seeds
2 teaspoons avocado oil
3 tablespoons brown rice
160 g shredded kale leaves
4 broccolini stalks
1 avocado, halved, stone removed
1 tablespoon hemp seeds
pinch of chilli flakes (optional)

Lemon–tamari dressing
2 tablespoons freshly squeezed lemon juice
1 tablespoon tamari or soy sauce

Preheat the oven to 180°C fan-forced. Line a baking tray with baking paper.

To make the dressing, whisk the lemon juice and tamari or soy sauce in a small bowl. Set aside.

Arrange the tofu on the prepared baking tray, sprinkle over the salt, pepper and sesame seeds and drizzle with half the oil. Bake for 35–40 minutes or until golden and crispy.

Meanwhile, cook the rice according to the packet instructions. Remove from the heat and set aside.

Heat the remaining oil in a large frying pan over medium heat and sauté the kale for 2 minutes or until slightly wilted. Transfer to serving bowls.

Add the broccolini to the pan and sauté for 3 minutes or until cooked through. Add to the bowls with the kale, along with the rice.

Toss everything together, then top with the baked tofu and half an avocado. Sprinkle over the hemp seeds and chilli flakes, if using. Drizzle with the dressing and serve.

JACKFRUIT NACHOS

Jackfruit is one of the ingredients I am most excited about right now, and you'll find a handful of recipes featuring it throughout this book. Young jackfruit has a stringy, pulled-pork-like texture and absorbs flavours really well. While jackfruit isn't the norm in Mexican cuisine, the fusion of Asian and Mexican ingredients in this recipe is absolutely delicious. Young jackfruit is sold in cans and it's becoming more accessible in Australia via health-food stores or online specialty stores. Asian supermarkets often stock it, too. For more information on jackfruit, see page 21.

Serves 2

150 g drained and rinsed canned young jackfruit
200 g drained and rinsed canned black beans
200 g canned diced tomatoes
½ red capsicum, diced
2 teaspoons harissa paste (or chilli sauce)
1 teaspoon smoked paprika
sea salt
1 avocado
juice of 1 lime
freshly ground black pepper
2 teaspoons chipotle sauce
3 tablespoons Cashew Cream Cheese (see page 282)
200 g corn chips

To serve

40 g (½ cup) finely shredded red cabbage
coriander leaves
pickled red onion (see page 286)
sliced pickled jalapeños
lime cheeks

• •

TIP

Use whole cans of jackfruit, beans and tomatoes if you're serving more than two people or if you'd like leftovers for the next day. You can use the extra mix to make more nachos or serve it with rice and salad.

• •

Place the jackfruit, black beans, tomatoes, capsicum, harissa and paprika in a saucepan over medium–high heat. Bring to the boil, then reduce the heat to medium and add 80 ml (⅓ cup) of water. Simmer, stirring occasionally, for 15 minutes. Season to taste with salt and mash the jackfruit using the back of a fork to break it up.

Meanwhile, mash the avocado with three-quarters of the lime juice and a pinch of salt and pepper.

Combine the chipotle sauce and cashew cream cheese in a small bowl and stir through 1–2 teaspoons of water and the remaining lime juice to loosen the mixture to a pouring consistency. Transfer to a serving bowl.

Construct your nachos on a serving platter. Start with a layer of corn chips, then spoon over the jackfruit and black bean mixture and smashed avocado. Top with the red cabbage, then scatter over a few coriander leaves and slices of pickled red onion and jalapeño. Drizzle over the chipotle cashew cream cheese and serve with lime cheeks.

SIMPLE DAL SOUP

My first cookbook featured a thick and hearty dal curry, but on my travels to India I discovered that dal comes in many forms. One of my favourite dishes was puri and dal, a soup-like dal served with freshly fried bread for dunking. Here is my version!

Serves 2

1 teaspoon melted coconut oil, plus extra to serve
1 teaspoon ground turmeric
1 teaspoon yellow mustard seeds
½ teaspoon sea salt
1 teaspoon freshly ground black pepper
220 g (1 cup) yellow split lentils
1 long green chilli, finely chopped
500 ml (2 cups) vegetable stock
½ teaspoon garam masala
coriander leaves, to serve
chilli flakes, to serve

Heat the oil in a saucepan over medium heat. Add the turmeric, mustard seeds, salt and pepper and sauté for 30 seconds or until the mustard seeds start to pop and crackle.

Add the lentils, chilli, stock and 1.25 litres of water to the pan and stir well. Reduce the heat to medium–low and gently simmer, covered and stirring occasionally, for about 1 hour or until the lentils are completely broken down and soft. You may need to add a little more water if the mixture is too thick.

Divide the soup between bowls, sprinkle over the garam masala, a pinch of salt and a good grinding of pepper. Top with a few coriander leaves and some chilli flakes and drizzle with a little extra coconut oil.

GREEK SALAD
WITH VEGAN HALOUMI

I always eat this dish when I visit Greece. You can order it without feta and the dressing is olive oil-based, making it a great vegan salad. Greek cuisine (and the Mediterranean diet in general) is highly revered for its health benefits and some of this is attributed to the amount of olive oil they use. I love olive oil and I use it in a lot of my cooking, but I also don't like to go too heavy on it, so for this salad I have kept the quantity lower than you would find in Greece.

This salad is great on its also but even better served with my vegan haloumi! Haloumi is a traditional Cypriot cheese that is very salty, with a firm, rubbery texture. I stumbled across the idea to create a vegan alternative while I was following a keto diet and experimenting with baked tofu. I discovered that when medium–firm tofu is baked, it has a taste and texture not dissimilar to haloumi, especially when sprinkled with salt and lemon juice. Of course, it's hard to exactly mimic that original haloumi texture, but this recipe comes pretty close to the real thing!

Serves 2
2 tomatoes, cut into wedges
10 kalamata or Sicilian olives
1 Lebanese cucumber, halved lengthways and
   cut into 1 cm thick slices
¼ red onion, finely sliced
1 teaspoon dried oregano
1 teaspoon olive oil
1 teaspoon red wine vinegar
1 teaspoon freshly squeezed lemon juice
pinch of sea salt
¼ teaspoon freshly ground black pepper
20 g Marinated Almond–Macadamia Feta
   (see page 270), cut into 1 cm chunks (optional)
lemon wedges, to serve

Vegan haloumi
300 g medium–firm tofu, cut into large
   1 cm thick triangles
1 tablespoon olive oil
1 teaspoon sea salt flakes
juice of ¼ lemon
chilli flakes, to serve (optional)

Preheat the oven to 200°C. Line a baking tray with baking paper.

To make the vegan haloumi, place the tofu on the prepared baking tray, drizzle with the oil and sprinkle the salt over the top. Bake for 20 minutes or until the edges of the tofu are golden.

Meanwhile, place the tomato, olives, cucumber and onion in a large salad bowl. Toss through the oregano, oil, vinegar, lemon juice, salt and pepper and place the almond feta on top, if desired. Set aside while you finish making the haloumi.

Preheat the grill to high, then grill the tofu for 5 minutes or until golden and crisp on top.

Transfer the vegan haloumi to serving plates and finish with the lemon juice and some chilli flakes (if using). Serve immediately with the Greek salad and lemon wedges.

BRUSSELS SPROUTS
WITH BAKON

This dish is a delicious way to get more veggies into your diet, plus it makes a fantastic side at family dinners. The inspiration came from my visit to New York where brussels sprouts are often served as a side dish with bacon crumbled on top. Ah-ha, I thought! Here is the perfect opportunity for me to veganise another classic. If brussels sprouts aren't your thing, don't turn the page just yet. Simply swap them out for broccoli florets and reduce the boiling time to 2 minutes.

Serves 2–3
350 g brussels sprouts, trimmed and halved
1 tablespoon olive oil, plus extra to serve
2 tablespoons slivered almonds
1 garlic clove, finely sliced
1 × quantity Konjac or Coconut Bakon (see page 289)
1 tablespoon chopped dill fronds
1 tablespoon freshly squeezed lemon juice,
 plus lemon wedges to serve
sea salt
chilli flakes, to serve

Bring a large saucepan of water to the boil. Add the brussels sprouts, then cover and boil for 5 minutes. Drain and set aside.

Heat the oil in a large non-stick frying pan over high heat. Add the brussels sprouts, almonds and garlic and sauté for 4 minutes or until the brussels are golden in parts.

Transfer to a serving plate and scatter over the konjac or coconut bakon and dill. Drizzle over the lemon juice and a little extra olive oil and sprinkle with salt and chilli flakes, to taste. Serve with lemon wedges.

Light meals

MEXICAN SALAD BOWL

This simple meal is perfect for when you feel like Mexican, but would prefer a lighter alternative to heavier dishes such as tacos and nachos. I love the addition of mango to this fresh Mexican-inspired bowl!

Serves 2 generously

110 g (½ cup) brown rice
400 g can black beans, top quarter of liquid drained
½ teaspoon sea salt
½ teaspoon onion powder
½ teaspoon ground cumin
¼ teaspoon chilli powder
1 sweetcorn cob, cut into 4 pieces
1 avocado
1 tablespoon freshly squeezed lime juice,
  plus lime wedges to serve
freshly ground black pepper
8 cos lettuce leaves, shredded
1 tomato, diced
1 mango cheek, flesh diced
small handful of coriander leaves, roughly chopped
chilli flakes, to serve
sliced fresh jalapeño, to serve

Lime and jalapeño dressing

2 tablespoons freshly squeezed lime juice
½ fresh jalapeño (or use sliced pickled jalapeños)
2 tablespoons apple cider vinegar
small handful of coriander leaves

Cook the rice according to the packet instructions, then remove from the heat and refresh under cold running water. Drain well, transfer to a bowl and set aside.

Meanwhile, place the black beans and their liquid, 125 ml (½ cup) of water, the salt, onion powder, cumin and chilli powder in a saucepan over medium–high heat. Simmer for 20–25 minutes or until thickened.

Dry-fry the corn in a frying pan over high heat for 4 minutes or until cooked through and charred on all sides.

In a bowl, roughly mash the avocado with the lime juice and a pinch of salt and pepper. Set aside.

To make the lime and jalapeño dressing, place the ingredients and 1 tablespoon of water in a blender and pulse until smooth. Add the dressing to the rice and stir through.

To serve, divide the rice, lettuce, tomato, mango, black beans, corn, mashed avocado and coriander between two bowls. Scatter over a few chilli flakes and sliced jalapeño and serve with lime wedges.

KALE CAESAR SALAD

When I visited New York, I became obsessed with the caesar at a cafe called The Butcher's Daughter, and I've been making it ever since. I love the addition of chickpeas and tempeh in this version.

Serves 2 generously
400 g can chickpeas
¼ teaspoon ground cumin
¼ teaspoon ground turmeric
¼ teaspoon smoked paprika
pinch of sea salt
1 teaspoon olive oil
80 g (2 cups) shredded kale leaves
80 g (2 cups) roughly chopped cos lettuce leaves
½ red onion, finely sliced
1 avocado, sliced

Tempeh bakon
¼ teaspoon smoked paprika
¼ teaspoon liquid smoke (see Tip)
2 teaspoons coconut aminos or tamari
1 teaspoon coconut sugar
pinch of sea salt
150 g tempeh, finely sliced

Caesar dressing
125 ml (½ cup) aquafaba (chickpea water
   from the can)
80 g (½ cup) cashews
juice of 1 lemon
1 teaspoon dijon mustard
2 garlic cloves
2 teaspoons capers, drained and rinsed
pinch of sea salt and freshly ground black pepper
1 tablespoon nutritional yeast flakes (optional)

Garlic bread
2 garlic cloves, crushed
2 slices sourdough
2 teaspoons olive oil

Drain and rinse the chickpeas, reserving the aquafaba (chickpea water) for the dressing. Place the chickpeas in a bowl, add the spices, salt and olive oil and toss together. Set aside.

To make the tempeh bakon, preheat the oven to 170°C fan-forced and line a baking tray with baking paper. Place all the ingredients except the tempeh in a bowl and stir. Add the tempeh and massage the sauce into each piece. Transfer to one side of the prepared tray in a single layer and sprinkle over some salt. Bake for 8 minutes, then add the chickpeas to the other side of the tray and bake for a further 20 minutes or until crisp.

Meanwhile, to make the dressing, blitz all the ingredients in a food processor until combined. Adjust the seasoning if necessary, then set aside.

To make the garlic bread, spread the garlic over the sourdough slices and drizzle over the oil. Transfer to a baking tray and bake for 3–4 minutes or until crisp. Set aside.

Heat a frying pan over high heat and sauté the kale for 1 minute or until wilted. Transfer to bowls, along with the lettuce and onion. Massage half the dressing into the salad, scatter over the bakon and chickpeas and top with the avocado and remaining dressing. Serve with the garlic bread.

• •

TIP
Liquid smoke can be bought online or from specialty food shops.

Light meals

WATERMELON CEVICHE
WITH COCONUT MILK

When I was in Mexico I tried a few variations of vegan ceviche. There, heart of palm was a popular ingredient, but I've struggled to find it back here in Australia. Having seen some fun poke bowl recipes using watermelon, I decided to add some to my ceviche, which makes it fresh, summery and zesty! This recipe also has similar ingredients to a watermelon gazpacho.

Serves 4
250 g watermelon, cut into 1.5 cm cubes
80 ml (⅓ cup) freshly squeezed lime juice
¼ teaspoon sea salt
1 avocado, diced
1 fresh jalapeño, finely sliced
½ green capsicum, diced
1 sweetcorn cob, kernels removed
125 ml (½ cup) coconut milk
1 tablespoon coconut aminos
small handful of coriander leaves
tortilla chips, to serve

Place the watermelon in a large bowl with the lime juice and salt. Toss together, then set aside to marinate for 15 minutes.

Add the remaining ingredients except the tortilla chips to the bowl. Spoon 3 tablespoons of water over the top and gently toss everything together.

Chill in the fridge for 15 minutes, then transfer to a shallow serving bowl and serve with tortilla chips on the side.

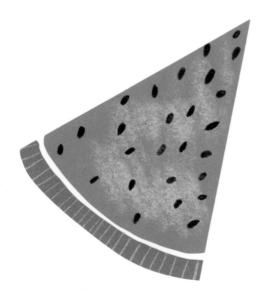

Light meals

MAINS

PAD THAI

WITH VEGAN SCRAMBLED EGGS

Pad thai is a popular Thai street-food dish, which traditionally contains shrimp paste, fish sauce and egg. Without these ingredients, I thought I would struggle to recreate its signature flavour, but during my travels in Thailand, I learned how to cook a vegan version that still packs a punch!

Serves 2
180 g pad thai rice noodles
1 tablespoon avocado or coconut oil
100 g firm tofu, cut into 1.5 cm thick batons
½ × quantity Vegan Scrambled Eggs (see page 46)
1 carrot, julienned
180 g (2 cups) bean sprouts
3 spring onions, cut into 3 cm lengths
juice of 1 lime, plus lime wedges to serve
3 tablespoons unsalted roasted peanuts,
  roughly chopped
1 teaspoon chilli powder

Pad thai sauce
3 tablespoons tamari or soy sauce
2 tablespoons coconut aminos
2 tablespoons tamarind paste
1–2 tablespoons coconut sugar
1 tablespoon Vegan Fish Sauce (see page 275)
  (optional)

To make the pad thai sauce, whisk all the ingredients and 3 tablespoons of water in a bowl. Set aside.

Bring a large saucepan of water to the boil. Add the noodles and cook for 2 minutes less than the packet instructions. Drain and refresh under cold running water.

Heat the oil in a wok over high heat. Add the tofu and sauté for 2 minutes, then add the drained noodles, vegan scrambled eggs and carrot and stir-fry for 1 minute. Add half the bean sprouts, half the spring onion and all the sauce. Continue to stir-fry for 1–2 minutes or until well combined and just cooked through.

Transfer the pad thai to shallow serving bowls and squeeze over the lime juice. Sprinkle the peanuts and chilli powder over the top and serve with the remaining bean sprouts, spring onion and the lime wedges on the side.

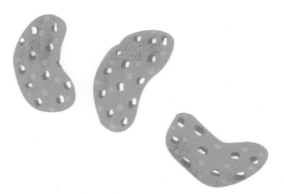

PINEAPPLE FRIED RICE

Adding pineapple to my fried rice is something I have always loved doing, so when I visited Thailand I was really excited to try authentic Thai fried rice with pineapple. If you want to add a wow factor to this dish, try serving it in hollowed-out pineapple halves, as I have here.

Serves 2

110 g (½ cup) brown rice
2 teaspoons avocado oil
1 large oyster mushroom, diced
sea salt
1 long red chilli, finely chopped
2 garlic cloves, finely chopped
1 teaspoon onion powder
½ teaspoon freshly ground black pepper
155 g (1 cup) frozen peas
1 pineapple, skin and core removed, flesh diced
155 g (1 cup) grated carrot
1 tablespoon tamari or soy sauce
200 g Vegan Scrambled Eggs (see page 46)
coriander leaves, to serve
lime wedges, to serve

Cook the rice according to the packet instructions, then remove from the heat and set aside.

Heat half the oil in a large frying pan or wok over high heat, add the mushroom and a pinch of salt and stir-fry for 2 minutes or until golden and crisp. Remove from the pan and set aside.

Return the pan to high heat and add the chilli, garlic, onion powder, ¼ teaspoon of salt, the pepper, peas, pineapple and cooked rice. Stir-fry for 1–2 minutes, then add the carrot, tamari or soy sauce and vegan scrambled eggs and fold together until well combined.

Transfer the mixture to serving bowls and top with the fried mushroom. Scatter over a few coriander leaves and serve with lime wedges on the side for squeezing over.

SPICY RAMEN

Inspired by my travels to South Korea, this spicy, salty and warming noodle soup will knock your socks off! Of course, if spice isn't your thing, no worries, just leave out the fiery sauce.

Serves 2 generously
sesame oil, for pan-frying
150 g medium tofu, cut into 1 cm cubes
1 teaspoon sesame seeds
100 g shiitake or oyster mushrooms, finely sliced
180 g ramen, soba or rice noodles
1 shallot, finely sliced
½ carrot, julienned
¼ red capsicum, julienned
1 head of bok choy, sliced

Ramen broth
1 litre vegetable stock
1½ teaspoons dried wakame (see Tip)
2–3 cm piece of ginger, sliced
2 garlic cloves, sliced
1 teaspoon freshly ground black pepper
2 tablespoons tamari or soy sauce
1–2 tablespoons Fiery Korean Sauce (see page 277), plus extra to serve

To serve
2 Vegan Fried Eggs (see page 44)
pinch of chilli powder (optional)
½ long red chilli, finely sliced
1 nori sheet, shredded
4 sorrel leaves
1 spring onion, sliced
Spicy Korean Kimchi (see page 284) (optional)

• •

TIP
You can purchase dried wakame from most Asian supermarkets, health-food stores or online.

Place the ramen broth ingredients and 250 ml (1 cup) of water in a large saucepan over medium–high heat and bring to a simmer.

Heat 1 teaspoon of sesame oil in a non-stick frying pan over high heat. Add the tofu and sesame seeds and sauté for 4–5 minutes or until the tofu is golden. Transfer to a plate and set aside. Add the mushroom and a little more sesame oil to the pan and fry for 4–5 minutes or until golden. Set aside with the sesame tofu.

Meanwhile, bring another saucepan of water to the boil and cook the noodles according to the packet instructions. Drain and rinse the noodles under cold running water and divide between serving bowls.

Add the shallot, carrot, capsicum and bok choy to the simmering broth, then reduce the heat to medium and simmer for 3–5 minutes or until the vegetables are just cooked through.

Ladle the broth and veggies into the noodle-filled bowls and add the tofu and mushroom. Add the fried eggs and sprinkle over a little chilli powder, if desired. Top with the sliced chilli, nori, sorrel and spring onion. Serve with a side of kimchi and extra fiery Korean sauce if you like it hot!

SINGAPOREAN LAKSA

Laksa is a creamy South East Asian noodle soup with origins in Singapore, Malaysia and Indonesia, but you will often find it on Thai menus as well. Malaysia and Singapore are both very close to Bali, so we have visited there often over the last two years. If you like making your own curry pastes, then you will love this dish! Freshly ground herbs and spices give this soup a huge flavour hit.

Serves 2 generously
2 teaspoons avocado oil
500 ml (2 cups) vegetable stock
1 tablespoon tamari or soy sauce
2 teaspoons coconut sugar
1 tablespoon Vegan Fish Sauce (see page 275)
  (optional)
100 g vermicelli noodles
boiling water
400 ml can coconut milk
200 g firm tofu, cut into 2 cm cubes
100 g snow peas, trimmed and halved lengthways
1 spring onion, finely sliced
juice of 1 lime

Laksa curry paste
2 teaspoons avocado oil
2 teaspoons sriracha chilli sauce
1 lemongrass stalk, white part only, finely sliced
  (or use 1 tablespoon lemongrass paste)
3 garlic cloves, roughly chopped
2–3 cm piece of ginger, roughly chopped
1 long red chilli, roughly chopped
2 tablespoons cleaned and roughly chopped
  coriander root
½ teaspoon ground coriander
¼ teaspoon ground cumin
½ teaspoon ground turmeric
¼ teaspoon freshly ground black pepper

To serve
90 g (1 cup) bean sprouts
handful of coriander leaves
1 tablespoon crispy fried shallots
¼ long red chilli, finely sliced (or 1 teaspoon
  sriracha chilli sauce) (optional)

To make the curry paste, place all the ingredients in a mortar and pound with a pestle for 5 minutes or until you have a smooth paste. Alternatively, you can make the paste in a food processor, although the flavour won't be quite the same.

Heat the oil in a wok over medium–high heat, add the curry paste and fry for 30 seconds or until fragrant. Add the stock, tamari or soy sauce, coconut sugar and vegan fish sauce (if using) and bring to a simmer.

Meanwhile, place the noodles in a large bowl, cover with boiling water and set aside for 2–3 minutes. Drain and rinse under cold running water, then transfer to serving bowls.

Reduce the wok heat to low, add the coconut milk, tofu, snow peas and half the spring onion. Simmer for 1 minute, then turn off the heat and stir through the lime juice.

Ladle the soup over the noodles and top with the remaining spring onion, bean sprouts, coriander leaves, fried shallots and fresh chilli or chilli sauce, if desired.

Mains

MASSAMAN CURRY

Massaman curry is typically made with slow-cooked beef, but during a recent trip to Thailand I was able to try a vegan version, and boy was it delicious! Massaman is a rich, creamy curry made with coconut cream and peanut butter. With the addition of warming spices, such as cardamom and cloves, it's also one of my favourites.

Serves 2

1 teaspoon avocado or coconut oil
1 all-purpose potato, cut into 1.5 cm cubes
200 g sweet potato, cut into 1.5 cm cubes
½ onion, quartered
¼ teaspoon sea salt
1 teaspoon tamarind paste
½ teaspoon ground turmeric
3 tablespoons chopped peanuts, plus extra to serve
1 teaspoon coconut sugar
1 tablespoon peanut butter
375 ml (1½ cups) coconut cream
80 g (½ cup) frozen peas
steamed jasmine rice, to serve

Massaman curry paste

5 long red chillies (or 4 long red and 1 bird's eye chilli
   if you like heat), roughly chopped, plus extra sliced
   chilli, to serve
½ teaspoon black peppercorns
2 teaspoons coriander seeds
½ teaspoon cumin seeds
½ teaspoon sea salt
½ teaspoon ground cinnamon
2 garlic cloves, roughly chopped
½ shallot, roughly chopped
3 cloves
2 cardamom pods
1 teaspoon finely chopped galangal
1 teaspoon finely chopped fresh turmeric
2 teaspoons cleaned and finely chopped
   coriander root

To make the curry paste, place the ingredients in a large mortar and pound with the pestle. Mix, pound and stir for 10 minutes or until you have a smooth, wet paste – you'll need to use quite a bit of force! (Alternatively, you can use a small food processor.)

Heat the oil in a large frying pan over high heat. Add 2 tablespoons of the curry paste and fry for 30 seconds, then add the potato, sweet potato and 250 ml (1 cup) of water. Cover and bring to the boil, then reduce the heat to medium and simmer for 6 minutes.

Add the onion, salt, tamarind paste, turmeric, chopped peanuts, coconut sugar, peanut butter and coconut cream and stir well. Simmer for 4 minutes, then check to see if the potato and sweet potato are cooked through. Add the peas and stir for 2 minutes.

Serve the curry in shallow bowls over rice, topped with extra chopped peanuts and red chilli.

Store the leftover curry paste in a jar in the fridge for up to 1 week.

MUSHROOM TACOS

Authentic tacos are very different to the old-school variety you find in Australia that feature minced beef, shredded tasty cheese, sour cream and a packet of taco sauce all served in a hard corn shell. When we were in Mexico, we didn't see any cheese or sour cream on the menu and hard taco shells were non-existent. Instead, they were served on freshly made corn tortillas with lots of fresh, local ingredients. I tried various vegan tacos while we were there, and I wanted to share my favourites in this book.

These mushroom tacos were inspired by some that we enjoyed at a hotel called La Valise during our honeymoon in Tulum. We sat by a beautiful beach in the afternoon, eating these delicious tacos and sipping margaritas. I've tried my best to recreate them here to bring you a true taste of Mexican cuisine.

Serves 2
160 g peeled and cored pineapple,
 cut into small triangles
2 large flat mushrooms, cut into 1 cm thick slices
sea salt
1 teaspoon chilli powder, or to taste
1 teaspoon coconut oil (optional)
½ avocado
1 tablespoon freshly squeezed lime juice,
 plus lime wedges to serve
pinch of freshly ground black pepper
4 soft corn tortillas (store-bought is fine)
2 tablespoons pickled red onion (see page 286)
1 tablespoon coconut aminos
coriander leaves, to serve
micro herbs, to serve (optional)

Heat a frying pan over medium–high heat and add the pineapple. Fry for 1–2 minutes on each side or until golden, then transfer to a plate and set aside.

Add the mushroom to the pan with 2 tablespoons of water, a pinch of salt and the chilli powder, and simmer until the liquid has evaporated. If you would like your mushroom to be golden and a little crispy, add the coconut oil to the pan and fry the mushroom slices for a further 2 minutes or until golden brown. Set aside.

Mash the avocado with the lime juice and a pinch of salt and pepper in a small bowl.

Fry the tortillas in a dry frying pan over high heat for 15 seconds on each side, then transfer to serving plates.

To assemble your tacos, spoon the mushroom mixture onto the tortillas and top with the grilled pineapple, mashed avocado and pickled red onion. Drizzle the coconut aminos over the tacos and scatter with a few coriander leaves and micro herbs (if using). Serve with lime wedges on the side.

Kalamari tacos

Mushroom tacos

Recipes
next page

Pumpkin & pesto tacos

PUMPKIN & PESTO
TACOS

This taco filling was inspired by another dish I ate in Mexico, which used baked pumpkin, crispy pumpkin seeds and a pumpkin seed pesto. I've added my marinated almond–macadamia feta to this recipe to make it even more delicious.

Serves 2

150 g peeled and deseeded pumpkin,
   cut into 1 cm cubes
1 tablespoon pumpkin seeds
2 teaspoons pure maple syrup
2 teaspoons olive oil
¼ teaspoon sea salt
pinch of ground cinnamon
4 soft corn tortillas (store-bought is fine)
2 tablespoons Marinated Almond–Macadamia
   Feta (see page 270)

Coriander and pumpkin seed pesto

1 kale stalk
½ cup coriander leaves
3 tablespoons pumpkin seeds
juice of ½ lime
1 tablespoon hemp seeds
¼ teaspoon sea salt
1 tablespoon olive oil

To serve

Crispy Pumpkin Seeds (see page 265)
pickled red onion (see page 286)
snow pea sprouts
lime wedges

Preheat the oven to 180°C fan-forced.

Place the pumpkin and pumpkin seeds in a bowl and drizzle over the maple syrup, oil, salt and cinnamon. Toss together and transfer to a small baking dish or tray. Bake for 25–30 minutes or until golden and crisp.

Meanwhile, make the pesto. Place all the ingredients and 3 tablespoons of water in a blender and blend until smooth. Transfer to a bowl and set aside.

Fry the tortillas in a dry frying pan over high heat for 15 seconds on each side, then transfer to serving plates.

To assemble your tacos, divide the baked pumpkin mixture among the tortillas and top with a teaspoon of pesto and a little crumbled feta. Scatter over some crispy pumpkin seeds, slices of pickled red onion and snow pea sprouts and serve with lime wedges on the side.

Any leftover pesto will keep in an airtight container in the fridge for up to 1 week.

KALAMARI TACOS

Many of the tacos served in coastal towns in Mexico celebrate fresh local seafood. I managed to find a vegan 'calamari' taco made with hearts of palm, but on returning home to Australia I couldn't find this ingredient anywhere, so I set out to find something that could replicate that chewy calamari texture. That's when I realised that konjac noodles would make a great substitute, as they have the perfect chewy texture.

Serves 2

½ avocado
1 tablespoon freshly squeezed lime juice,
  plus lime wedges to serve
sea salt and freshly ground black pepper
35 g tapioca flour
100 g thick konjac noodles (see Tip),
  cut into 2–3 cm lengths
1½ tablespoons avocado oil
30 g (½ cup) panko breadcrumbs
4 soft corn tortillas (store-bought is fine)
60 g Cashew Cream Cheese (see page 282)
75 g (1 cup) finely shredded red cabbage
½ fresh jalapeño, sliced
micro herbs, to serve (optional)

• •

TIP
You can find konjac noodles at most Asian supermarkets.

• •

In a bowl, mash the avocado with the lime juice and season to taste with salt and pepper. Set aside.

Place the tapioca flour and 1 tablespoon of water in a bowl and stir to make a runny mixture. Place the konjac noodles in the bowl and toss through to coat. Sprinkle over ¼ teaspoon of salt and ½ teaspoon of pepper and toss again.

Heat the oil in a frying pan or wok over medium–high heat.

Place the panko breadcrumbs on a plate and toss through the konjac noodles until completely coated. Place the crumbed noodles in the hot oil and fry, turning frequently, for 3–4 minutes or until golden all over. Transfer to a plate lined with paper towel to drain any excess oil.

Fry the tortillas in a dry frying pan over high heat for 15 seconds on each side, then transfer to serving plates.

Spread the cashew cream cheese over the tacos and top with the shredded cabbage, kalamari and dollops of mashed avocado. Finish with jalapeño slices, a few micro herbs (if using), extra salt and pepper and lime wedges for squeezing over.

KOREAN SUSHI

During my travels in South Korea, my sister and I attended a fantastic Korean cooking class. One of the dishes we made was Korean sushi, or gimbap. The difference between gimbap and Japanese sushi is the addition of pickled veg, kimchi and sesame seeds. It's then served with a spicy dipping sauce.

Serves 2

80 g tempeh, sliced into thin strips
2 tablespoons Fiery Korean Sauce (see page 277), plus extra to serve (see Tip)
1 tablespoon sesame oil
550 g (3 cups) cooked brown rice
3 nori sheets
6 pickled daikon batons or any pickled veg (see page 286)
3 tablespoons Spicy Korean Kimchi (see page 284)
½ avocado, finely sliced
2 teaspoons sesame seeds
sorrel leaves, to serve (optional)

• • • • • • • • • • • • • • • • • • • •

TIP

If you don't like it spicy, just use soy sauce for dipping.

• • • • • • • • • • • • • • • • • • • •

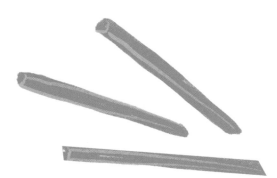

Place the tempeh and fiery Korean sauce in a small bowl, mix well and set aside for 20–30 minutes to marinate.

Stir half the sesame oil through the cooked rice and set aside.

Heat a frying pan over medium heat, add the tempeh and fry for 1 minute on each side or until golden. Set aside.

Lay a nori sheet on a bamboo sushi mat and spread with a thin layer of rice, leaving a 2.5 cm border. Place a few strips of tempeh along the centre of the rice and top with two pieces of pickled veg, 1 tablespoon of the kimchi and a few slices of avocado. Dab a little water along the top edge of the nori sheet and roll up as you would a sushi roll, using the bamboo mat to assist you. Repeat with the remaining nori sheets and filling.

Brush the rolls with the remaining sesame oil, sprinkle over the sesame seeds and refrigerate for 20 minutes.

Once chilled, use a sharp knife to cut each roll into four to six even pieces. Serve with the fiery dipping sauce and a few sorrel leaves scattered over the top, if desired.

PAD SEE EW

This Thai dish is made with thick flat rice noodles and a sweet soy sauce. I learned how to make it in Thailand and discovered that it contains loads of sugar, so here I've created a healthier version.

Serves 2 generously

3 tablespoons cashews
3 teaspoons avocado or coconut oil
100 g firm tofu, cut into 1 cm × 3 cm rectangles
3 broccolini stalks, roughly chopped
10 snow peas, trimmed
½ red capsicum, finely sliced
6 baby sweetcorn spears
450 g fresh thick flat rice noodles (see Tip)
small handful of Thai basil leaves, to serve
lime cheeks, to serve

Pad see ew sauce

1 long green chilli, chopped (deseeded if you prefer less heat)
2 garlic cloves, chopped
2 tablespoons tamari or soy sauce
1 teaspoon coconut sugar
1 tablespoon tomato paste
3 tablespoons Thai basil leaves

• •

TIP

You can find fresh thick flat rice noodles in the fresh section at your local Asian supermarket.

• •

To make the pad see ew sauce, pound the chilli and garlic using a mortar and pestle to make a paste. Add the rest of the ingredients and 3 tablespoons of water and mix well to combine. Set aside.

Dry-fry the cashews in a wok or frying pan over medium heat until golden. Remove from the pan and set aside.

Place the pan back on the stovetop, increase the heat to high and add 1 teaspoon of the oil. Add the tofu and stir-fry for 2–3 minutes or until golden on all sides. Remove from the pan and set aside with the cashews.

Add the remaining oil to the pan, along with the broccolini, snow peas, capsicum and baby sweetcorn. Stir-fry for 1 minute, then add the noodles and cooked tofu and stir-fry for another minute. Pour over the sauce and stir-fry for a further minute or so.

Transfer the pad see ew to serving bowls, top with the reserved cashews and the Thai basil leaves and serve with lime cheeks on the side for squeezing over.

LEMONGRASS TOFU
STIR-FRY

I learned how to make this super easy and delicious stir-fry in a cooking class in Vietnam. It makes a perfect quick and healthy dinner! Serve with a side of morning glory (see page 84) for extra greens.

Serves 2

avocado or coconut oil, for frying
250 g firm tofu, cut into 1 cm thick triangles
220 g (1 cup) brown rice
1 spring onion, finely sliced
1 carrot, julienned
½ red capsicum, finely sliced
2 garlic cloves, finely sliced
1 tablespoon crispy fried shallots, to serve (optional)
mixed herbs, such as mint, coriander and
    Thai basil, to serve
lime cheeks, to serve

Lemongrass marinade

125 ml (½ cup) vegetable stock
1 lemongrass stalk, white part only, finely sliced
1 tablespoon crushed garlic
1 tablespoon coconut sugar
2 tablespoons tamari or soy sauce
1 long red chilli (or 1 bird's eye chilli if you like it spicy),
    finely chopped
2–3 cm piece of ginger, finely chopped
1 teaspoon freshly ground black pepper
2 teaspoons tapioca flour

Heat 2 teaspoons of oil in a large frying pan or wok over medium heat, add the tofu and fry for 1 minute on each side or until golden. Remove from the pan and set aside.

To make the lemongrass marinade, combine all the ingredients in a large bowl. If you have a mortar and pestle, you can pound the ingredients to break down the spices and release more aromas. Add the tofu and place in the fridge to marinate for 30–60 minutes.

Meanwhile, cook the rice according to the packet instructions. Remove from the heat and set aside.

Heat 2 teaspoons of oil in the frying pan or wok over high heat. Add the spring onion, carrot and capsicum and stir-fry for 2 minutes, then add the tofu and marinade and stir-fry for a further 3 minutes.

In a separate frying pan, heat ½ teaspoon of oil over medium heat. Add the garlic and fry for 1 minute, then remove from the heat and spoon over the rice.

Divide the garlic rice between bowls and top with the tofu and vegetables. Sprinkle over the crispy fried shallots (if using) and top with the herbs. Serve with lime cheeks for squeezing over.

KOREAN BIBIMBAP

Bibimbap is my favourite Korean dish as, essentially, it's a big beautiful Buddha bowl! It's packed with healthy ingredients, but I particularly love the pickled veg in this dish. Koreans have a strong focus on beauty and health, and many of the current health-food and herbal medicine trends stem from Korea. Fermented veggies, such as kimchi, contain both prebiotics and probiotics, which are great for digestion, healthy gut flora and increasing absorption of micronutrients.

Serves 2
185 g (1 cup) cooked brown rice
50 g Chinese spinach or kale, finely chopped
2 teaspoons sesame oil
100 g king oyster or shiitake mushrooms, finely sliced
2 teaspoons sesame seeds
pinch of sea salt
½ cup pickled carrot, daikon and cucumber
  (see page 286)
½ nashi pear, cored and cut into cubes
50 g (½ cup) bean sprouts
1 avocado, halved, stone removed
3 tablespoons Spicy Korean Kimchi (see page 284)
2 nori sheets, roughly chopped
½ spring onion, finely sliced
2 Vegan Fried Eggs (see page 44)
micro herbs, to serve (optional)
1–2 tablespoons Fiery Korean Sauce (see page 277)

Divide the rice between two serving bowls.

Set a steamer over a saucepan of boiling water and steam the Chinese spinach or kale for 2 minutes. Add to the serving bowls.

Heat the sesame oil in a frying pan over high heat and add the mushroom, sesame seeds and salt. Sauté for 3–4 minutes or until golden, then transfer to the serving bowls.

Add the pickled carrot, daikon and cucumber, nashi and bean sprouts, along with the avocado.

Top the bowls with the kimchi, nori, spring onion, fried eggs and a few micro herbs (if using). Pour the fiery sauce over the top, stir everything together and enjoy!

SMOKED JACKFRUIT TACOS

These tacos combine some of my favourite Mexican and Vietnamese flavours. This recipe was inspired by the eggplant tacos at Leeroy's Vietnamese restaurant in Canggu, Bali. I fell in love with them and they're a must-try if you're in the region!

Makes 6

2 teaspoons avocado oil
400 g can young jackfruit, drained and rinsed, roughly chopped
1 teaspoon smoked paprika
1 tablespoon finely diced red onion
2 teaspoons chipotle sauce
2 tablespoons tomato paste
¼ teaspoon five spice powder
6 small soft flour tortillas
75 g (1 cup) finely shredded red cabbage
1 carrot, julienned

Tamari–maple sauce

2 tablespoons tamari or soy sauce
1 tablespoon pure maple syrup
1 teaspoon sriracha chilli sauce

To serve

handful of coriander leaves
2 tablespoons crispy fried shallots
1 teaspoon chilli powder
lime wedges

Heat the oil in a frying pan over medium heat. Add the jackfruit, paprika and red onion and sauté for 1 minute. Add the chipotle sauce, tomato paste, five spice powder and 3 tablespoons of water and simmer, stirring occasionally, for 8 minutes or until the jackfruit is soft and cooked through. Break up the jackfruit using the back of a fork so that it appears 'shredded'.

Meanwhile, combine all the tamari–maple sauce ingredients in a small bowl. Set aside.

Fry the tortillas in a dry frying pan over high heat for 15 seconds on each side, then transfer to serving plates.

To assemble the tacos, divide the cabbage, carrot and jackfruit mixture among the tortillas. Top with a few coriander leaves, crispy fried shallots and a good pinch of chilli powder. Drizzle over the tamari–maple sauce and serve with lime wedges on the side.

NASI GORENG

This classic Indonesian dish doesn't often make its way onto restaurant menus or home dinner tables, so I really wanted to make a delicious vegan version that can be enjoyed away from the Bali beachside warungs and street carts!

Serves 2 generously
190 g (1 cup) red rice
250 g cauliflower florets
2 teaspoons coconut oil
¼ teaspoon sea salt
100 g green beans, trimmed
1 spring onion, finely sliced
1 long red chilli, finely sliced

Nasi goreng sauce
1–2 teaspoons sambal olek
1 tablespoon tomato paste
3 tablespoons coconut aminos
3 garlic cloves, crushed
1 teaspoon onion powder
2 tablespoons freshly squeezed lime juice

Tempeh skewers
1 teaspoon coconut oil
100 g tempeh, cut into 2 cm cubes
2 teaspoons coconut aminos

To serve
2 Vegan Fried Eggs (see page 44)
6 plain rice crackers
1 tablespoon crispy fried shallots
3 tablespoons pickled carrot and cucumber
  (see page 286)
2 tablespoons crushed unsalted roasted peanuts

Cook the rice according to the packet instructions, then remove from the heat and set aside.

Meanwhile, to make the nasi goreng sauce, combine all the ingredients in a bowl and set aside.

To make the tempeh skewers, heat the oil in a frying pan over medium heat. Add the tempeh and fry for 30 seconds on each side or until golden. Transfer to a bowl and drizzle over the coconut aminos. Toss together and set aside.

Grate or blitz the cauliflower in a food processor until finely chopped.

Heat the oil in a frying pan over high heat and add the cooked rice and cauliflower. Sauté, tossing well, for 1 minute, then add the salt, beans, spring onion and chilli and stir-fry for 30 seconds. Add the nasi goreng sauce and stir-fry for a further 30 seconds.

Spoon the rice into two serving bowls. Thread the tempeh onto bamboo skewers and place on top of the fried rice with the fried eggs, rice crackers, fried shallots, pickled veg and peanuts.

BAKED MAC-NO-CHEESE

The mac-no-cheese recipe in my first cookbook turned out to be the most popular dish. It was amazing to hear from so many people who cooked and loved the recipe, whether they made it for their family, friends or just themselves. It's a truly delicious meal, so I wanted to share a fun, new version in this book, inspired by my travels in the United States where mac 'n' cheese is on menus everywhere. I noticed that bacon was often added to the dish, so I've added coconut bacon to this recipe to give it a special twist.

Serves 4

250 g macaroni
350 g peeled and deseeded pumpkin,
  roughly chopped
3 tablespoons nutritional yeast flakes
3 tablespoons soy or almond milk
1 teaspoon freshly ground black pepper
½ teaspoon sea salt
1 teaspoon onion powder
1 teaspoon garlic powder
2 teaspoons olive oil
3 tablespoons cashews
100 g cauliflower florets
100 g broccoli florets
2 tablespoons Coconut Bakon (see page 289)
2 tablespoons Parmesan Crumble (see page 265)

Preheat the oven to 160°C fan-forced.

Bring a saucepan of salted water to the boil and cook the pasta according to the packet instructions. Drain and rinse under cold running water, then set aside.

Meanwhile, bring another saucepan of water to the boil, add the pumpkin and cook for 8–10 minutes or until tender. Drain and transfer the pumpkin to a blender, along with the nutritional yeast flakes, soy or almond milk, pepper, salt, onion powder, garlic powder, oil and cashews. Blend on high until smooth.

Refill the saucepan with water and bring to the boil again. Add the cauliflower and cook for 3 minutes, then add the broccoli and cook for a further 2 minutes. Drain and place in a baking dish.

Add the pasta to the baking dish and pour over the pumpkin sauce. Mix well so that the pasta is fully coated.

Sprinkle over the coconut bakon and parmesan crumble and bake for 20 minutes or until golden. Remove from the oven and allow to cool for 5 minutes before serving.

THE BOSS BURRITO

A burrito is a large flour tortilla filled with a protein, rice and salad. Burritos are generally only eaten in the north of Mexico, but we did find this awesome burrito shop called Burrito Amor in Tulum, which is in the south. They made a vegan burrito with the most delicious chipotle sauce, and this is my interpretation.

Makes 3

110 g (½ cup) brown rice
400 g can black beans, top quarter of liquid drained
250 ml (1 cup) vegetable stock
1 teaspoon ground cumin
sea salt
1 tomato, diced
3 tablespoons coriander, finely chopped
¼ red onion, finely diced
juice of 1 lime
1 avocado
freshly ground black pepper
3 tablespoons Cashew Cream Cheese (see page 282)
2 teaspoons chipotle sauce, plus extra for drizzling (optional)
40 g (1 cup) finely shredded kale leaves
75 g (1 cup) finely shredded red cabbage
3 large flour tortillas
2 tablespoons pickled jalapeño slices

Cook the rice according to the packet instructions. Remove from the heat and set aside.

Meanwhile, place the beans and liquid, vegetable stock, cumin and ⅓ teaspoon of salt in a saucepan over medium heat. Simmer for about 30 minutes or until reduced.

Place the tomato, coriander, red onion and half the lime juice in a bowl, mix well and set aside.

In another bowl, mash the avocado with the remaining lime juice and season well.

In a third bowl, combine the cashew cream cheese with the chipotle sauce.

Finally, toss together the kale and cabbage.

Preheat a sandwich press. Lay each tortilla on a large square of foil.

Spread the cashew cream cheese over the tortillas and spoon the rice and bean mixture down the centre. Top with the kale and cabbage, tomato mixture, avocado and jalapeños. If you like chipotle sauce, drizzle a little more over.

To fold your burritos, tuck both sides in first, then carefully fold the end nearest to you over the filling and roll up tightly. Wrap in foil and transfer to the sandwich press for 60 seconds or until warmed through (you can also eat the burritos fresh if you don't have a sandwich press). If you don't wrap your burritos in foil, they will toast in the sandwich press, giving you a crispier finish.

BANH XEO

This delicious crispy Vietnamese pancake is infused with turmeric, studded with chunks of tofu and mushroom and served with an abundance of fresh herbs and my tangy nuoc cham. Banh xeo was my absolute favourite street-food dish when I was in Vietnam. To my delight, the banh xeo pancake batter doesn't contain any egg; however, the pancake itself is usually filled with prawn and pork, so I decided to make a vegan version.

Serves 2

175 g (1 cup) rice flour
125 ml (½ cup) coconut milk
   (shake well before opening
   the can)
1 teaspoon sea salt
pinch of freshly ground
   black pepper
1 teaspoon ground turmeric
1 tablespoon nutritional
   yeast flakes
1 spring onion, finely sliced
olive oil, for frying
100 g medium tofu, finely diced
2 shiitake mushrooms (or any
   mushrooms you have on hand),
   finely sliced
¼ teaspoon five spice powder
180 g (2 cups) bean sprouts
200 g mustard greens or
   8 cos lettuce leaves
1 cup mixed herbs, such as shiso,
   Vietnamese mint, Thai basil and
   coriander
4–6 rice paper sheets
80 ml (⅓ cup) Nuoc Cham
   (see page 278)
lime cheeks, to serve

Whisk the rice flour, coconut milk, 375 ml (1½ cups) of water, salt, pepper, turmeric, nutritional yeast flakes and green spring onion in a bowl. Set aside to rest for 30 minutes.

Meanwhile, heat 2 teaspoons of oil in a frying pan over medium heat. Add the tofu, mushroom and five spice powder and fry for 2–3 minutes or until the mushroom and tofu are golden. Transfer to a plate and set aside.

Place the bean sprouts in a bowl next to the stovetop. Prepare a serving plate with the mustard greens or lettuce, herbs and rice paper. You will also need a clean wet cloth to dampen the rice paper just before serving. Pour the nuoc cham into two small ramekins.

To make the pancakes, place a non-stick frying pan over medium–high heat and wait for it to get hot. Add 1 teaspoon of oil and toss in a few slices of the white spring onion, along with a spoonful of the tofu and mushroom. Allow to sizzle for 10 seconds, then pour in approximately 80 ml (⅓ cup) of batter, swirling the pan to evenly coat the base – you should immediately begin to see air bubbles.

Cover with a lid and cook for 30 seconds, then remove the lid and toss in a small handful of bean sprouts. Replace the lid and continue to cook for 1 minute or until the pancake edge is golden and crisp. Fold over one half of the pancake to form a semi-circle and fry for a further 15 seconds, then transfer to a plate.

The pancakes are best eaten straight away, so you may like to eat as you go along. To eat, moisten a rice paper sheet with a wet cloth, then tear a strip of it off and place a lettuce leaf on top. Tear off a piece of the pancake and place it on the lettuce leaf, then top with a few herbs and a squeeze of lime. Use the rice paper sheet to wrap it all up and dunk in the tangy nuoc cham.

Continue with the remaining batter and ingredients.

BEAN RENDANG BURGERS

My favourite vegan restaurant in Bali is Peloton Supershop in Berawa, where you can also find some of my signature recipes on the menu. They make a delicious rendang jackfruit burger, which is the inspiration for this recipe. I decided to give my patties their own spin by using sweet potato, eggplant and kidney beans as they're readily available.

Serves 4

250 g sweet potato, cut into
   2 cm cubes
3 teaspoons avocado oil
1 onion, finely diced
2 garlic cloves, crushed
100 g eggplant, cut into
   1 cm cubes
100 g rendang paste (see Tip)
1 tablespoon tamari or soy sauce
1 tablespoon coconut aminos
pinch of sea salt
400 g can kidney beans, drained
   and rinsed

Slaw

75 g (1 cup) finely shredded
   red cabbage
½ carrot, julienned
2 tablespoons Sriracha Mayo
   (see page 282)

To serve

4 sourdough buns
1 tomato, sliced
small handful of coriander leaves
⅓ cup snow pea sprouts
2 tablespoons coconut aminos

Bring a saucepan of water to the boil, add the sweet potato and boil for 8 minutes or until cooked through. Drain and set aside.

Meanwhile, heat 1 teaspoon of the oil in a frying pan over medium–high heat. Add the onion and garlic and sauté for 2 minutes, then add the eggplant and rendang paste and sauté for 5 minutes. Add the sweet potato and gently mash with the back of a fork. Stir through the tamari or soy sauce, coconut aminos and salt, then stir in the beans and cook for a further 3 minutes or until the eggplant has softened and easily breaks apart when tested with a knife. Remove from the heat and allow to cool.

Preheat the oven to 180°C fan-forced. Line a baking tray with baking paper.

Shape the mixture into four even-sized patties and place on the prepared tray. Bake for 20 minutes (this helps to retain their shape).

Heat the remaining oil in a frying pan and cook the patties for 1–2 minutes on each side to really crisp them up.

To make the slaw, combine the cabbage, carrot and mayo in a bowl.

Cut the buns in half and pile the slaw onto the bottom half of each bun. Top with tomato, a patty, coriander leaves and sprouts. Drizzle over the coconut aminos and top with the other half of the bun.

• •

TIP

You can find rendang paste in the Asian section of supermarkets. Check the ingredients list to make sure it's vegan, as some pastes contain fish sauce and/or shrimp paste.

VEGETABLE
&
CHICKPEA STEW WITH COUSCOUS

This simple chickpea stew reminds me of my travels to Turkey and the Middle East, where dates are often added to savoury dishes to add sweetness, along with chickpeas for protein. I especially love serving this with couscous as it only takes five minutes to prepare!

Serves 2 generously
½ red onion, sliced
1 teaspoon ground cumin
1 teaspoon smoked paprika
2–3 cm piece of ginger, finely chopped
750 ml (3 cups) vegetable stock
400 g can diced tomatoes
250 g sweet potato, cut into 2 cm cubes
1 carrot, cut into 2 cm pieces
400 g can chickpeas, drained and rinsed (see Tip)
5 medjool dates, pitted and chopped
95 g (½ cup) couscous
125 ml (½ cup) boiling water
1 tablespoon olive oil
chopped coriander leaves, to serve
sea salt and freshly ground black pepper

. . . .

TIP
Keep your chickpea liquid (aquafaba) to make the sriracha mayo on page 282 or the caesar dressing on page 110.

. . . .

Heat a large saucepan over medium–high heat and add the onion, cumin, paprika, ginger, stock, tomatoes and sweet potato. Simmer for 15 minutes, then add the carrot, chickpeas and dates. Reduce the heat to low and simmer for a further 15 minutes or until the vegetables are cooked through and the liquid has reduced to a stew-like consistency.

Meanwhile, place the couscous in a bowl and cover with the boiling water. Cover the bowl with a plate or a saucepan lid and set aside for 5 minutes. Fluff the couscous with a fork and drizzle over the olive oil. Stir through to combine and transfer the couscous to a serving plate.

Spoon the stew over the couscous and sprinkle over the coriander. Season with salt and pepper and serve straight away.

MOUSSAKA

If you've never tried moussaka, think of it as a lasagne crossed with shepherd's pie. Typically, it contains meat, but you can often find vegetarian versions in Greek restaurants. Unfortunately, they are not vegan because of the dairy in the creamy white sauce, so I created this dairy-free version to satisfy my cravings.

Serves 4–6

2 teaspoons olive oil
1 onion, finely diced
2 garlic cloves, crushed
1 dried bay leaf
¼ teaspoon ground cinnamon
1 teaspoon dried oregano
400 g can lentils, drained
  and rinsed
sea salt
pinch of freshly ground
  black pepper
400 g can diced tomatoes
2 tablespoons tomato paste
150 ml red wine
360 g eggplant, cut into 1 cm
  thick slices
350 g all-purpose potatoes,
  cut into 1 cm thick slices
pinch of ground nutmeg
1 tablespoon Parmesan Crumble
  (see page 265)
Greek Salad (see page 102),
  to serve

White sauce

1 tablespoon vegan butter
250 ml (1 cup) soy milk
1 tablespoon nutritional
  yeast flakes
pinch of sea salt
2 tablespoons plain flour

Preheat the oven to 180°C fan-forced.

Heat half the oil in a saucepan over medium–high heat. Add the onion, garlic, bay leaf, cinnamon, oregano, lentils and a pinch of salt and pepper and sauté for 2–3 minutes or until the onion is soft. Add the tomatoes, tomato paste and red wine. Reduce the heat to low, then cover and simmer, stirring occasionally, for 6 minutes.

Meanwhile, place the eggplant on a chopping board, sprinkle both sides with 2 teaspoons of salt and allow to sit for 10 minutes (this helps to soften and remove any bitterness). Rinse the eggplant in a colander, then drain well and pat dry with paper towel.

Bring a saucepan of salted water to the boil, add the potato and boil for 4–6 minutes or until just undercooked. Drain and set aside.

To make the white sauce, heat the vegan butter, soy milk, nutritional yeast flakes and salt in a small saucepan over medium heat. Whisk together, then sift in the flour 2 teaspoons at a time, whisking constantly and incorporating the flour into the sauce before adding more. Continue to whisk until the sauce thickens to a creamy consistency, then remove from the heat and set aside.

Now it's time to build your moussaka. Spoon one-third of the lentil mixture over the base of a large baking dish, followed by a layer of half the potato and half the eggplant (gaps between the vegetables are fine). Spoon over another third of the lentil mixture and spread evenly. Continue with the remaining potato and the remaining lentil mixture, and finish with the eggplant. Pour over the white sauce, spreading it evenly across the top, then sprinkle over the nutmeg.

Bake for 35–40 minutes, then sprinkle over the parmesan crumble and return to the oven for 5 minutes or until golden and bubbling.

Serve the moussaka in shallow bowls with a side of Greek salad.

MEAT-LESS MEATBALLS

These flavour-packed vegan meatballs are made using kidney beans for a protein kick. Dunked in passata sauce and served with pasta, they make a hearty main, but on their own they also make a great healthy snack or lunchbox filler.

Serves 2
cooked spaghetti, to serve
Parmesan Crumble (see page 265), to serve

Meatballs
3 tablespoons red or white quinoa
1 portobello mushroom, roughly chopped
400 g can red kidney beans, drained and rinsed
30 g plain or gluten-free flour
1½ teaspoons onion powder
½ teaspoon garlic powder
½ teaspoon sea salt
½ teaspoon freshly ground black pepper
2 teaspoons finely chopped flat-leaf parsley leaves
1 tomato, deseeded and finely diced

Tomato sauce
250 ml (1 cup) passata
⅓ cup basil leaves, plus extra to serve
sea salt and freshly ground black pepper

• •

TIPS
You can also serve the meatballs and sauce as a tapas-style dish with the parmesan crumble.

If you prefer, you can shallow-fry the meatballs. Heat 3 tablespoons of avocado oil in a frying pan over medium heat. Add the meatballs and cook for 2–3 minutes on all sides or until golden and crispy.

• •

Preheat the oven to 180°C. Line a baking tray with baking paper.

To make the meatballs, cook the quinoa according to the packet instructions, then drain and set aside to cool.

Place the mushroom and kidney beans in the bowl of a food processor and process until just combined. Transfer to a large bowl and stir through the quinoa. Add the remaining ingredients and mix well.

Roll the mixture into ten even-sized balls, then place on the prepared tray and bake for 18–20 minutes or until cooked through.

To make the tomato sauce, heat the passata in a saucepan over medium heat. Add the basil and salt and pepper to taste, then simmer for 5 minutes.

Divide the spaghetti between two plates and top with the meatballs and sauce. Scatter over the parmesan crumble and extra basil leaves.

BANH MI

The history of this famous Vietnamese sandwich can be traced back to the French colonisation of Vietnam, when the country was first introduced to the baguette, pâté and mayonnaise. Typically, banh mi contains processed meat, but I was lucky enough to find an amazing vegan version in Hoi An so I could see what all the fuss was about! Crusty bread packed with pickled veg, herbs and saucy tofu – it was delicious. These make for a great portable lunch or picnic dinner.

Serves 2

2 teaspoons olive oil
100 g firm tofu, cut into 1 cm thick strips
2 shiitake mushrooms, finely sliced
¼ teaspoon five spice powder
2 Vietnamese rolls or small baguettes
1 tablespoon olive tapenade
3 tablespoons pickled jalapeño slices
⅓ cup pickled carrot and cucumber (see page 286)
1 cup mixed herbs, such as Vietnamese mint, Thai basil and coriander
2 tablespoons Sriracha Mayo (see page 282)

Marinade

⅓ lemongrass stalk, white part only, roughly chopped
2 tablespoons tamari or soy sauce
1 teaspoon coconut sugar
2 garlic cloves, crushed
½ long red chilli, chopped
2 tablespoons Nuoc Cham (see page 278)

Heat half the oil in a frying pan over medium heat, add the tofu and cook for 1 minute on each side or until golden. Remove the tofu from the pan and place in a bowl.

Next, place the marinade ingredients in a blender and blend until well combined. Pour the marinade over the tofu and set aside in the fridge for at least 30 minutes (the longer you leave it to marinate, the better).

Heat the remaining oil in a frying pan over medium heat. Add the mushroom and five spice powder and sauté for 3 minutes or until the mushroom is golden. Remove from the pan and set aside.

Slice open the rolls or baguettes, but don't cut all the way through. Spread the olive tapenade on one side of the bread and divide the marinated tofu and mushroom between the rolls. Spoon 1 tablespoon of the marinade over the tofu for extra flavour and stuff the jalapeño slices, pickled carrot and cucumber and herbs inside each roll. Finish with a drizzle of sriracha mayo. Eat straight away or pack for a yummy picnic lunch!

Any leftover marinade can be stored in an airtight container in the fridge for up to 1 week. Use it for your next banh mi session or as a stir-fry sauce.

PANANG CURRY

Panang is my husband Alex's favourite Thai curry. It is similar to a red curry, but milder and creamier. For this dish I've added pumpkin, tofu and Thai eggplant, as I love the way these ingredients soak up the delicious curry flavours.

Serves 2

200 g peeled and deseeded pumpkin, cut into 3 cm chunks
4 Thai eggplants
1 tablespoon avocado oil
100 g medium tofu, cut into 2 cm cubes
½ onion, cut into 1 cm chunks
2 kaffir lime leaves
250 ml (1 cup) coconut cream
1 tablespoon Vegan Fish Sauce (see page 275) (optional)
1–2 tablespoons tamari or soy sauce
1 teaspoon coconut sugar
1 tablespoon peanut butter (optional)
½ cup Thai basil leaves, plus extra to serve
steamed jasmine rice or cooked rice noodles, to serve

Panang curry paste

1 lemongrass stalk, white part only
2 garlic cloves
1 shallot, quartered
½ teaspoon cumin seeds
1 teaspoon coriander seeds
5 long red chillies, roughly chopped, plus extra, sliced, to serve
3 cm piece of galangal, finely chopped
3 tablespoons coriander roots, scraped clean and chopped
1 cm piece of fresh turmeric
2 kaffir lime leaves, shredded
½ teaspoon sea salt
2 tablespoons crushed peanuts

First, make the curry paste. Smash the lemongrass, garlic and shallot with the flat edge of a knife. Place the cumin and coriander seeds in a mortar and grind to a powder with a pestle. Add the lemongrass, garlic and shallot, along with the remaining paste ingredients except the peanuts, and pound for 10 minutes or until the mixture forms a paste. Add the peanuts and pound until well combined. (Alternatively, you could use a blender, but you may need to add a dash of water or oil to help keep the ingredients moving.)

Bring a large saucepan of water to the boil, add the pumpkin and eggplants and boil for 10 minutes or until cooked through. Drain and set aside.

Heat the oil in a frying pan or wok over high heat, add 1–2 tablespoons of curry paste and fry for 30 seconds or until aromatic. Add the tofu, onion, pumpkin, eggplants, kaffir lime leaves, coconut cream and 125 ml (½ cup) of water. Reduce the heat to medium and simmer for 15 minutes.

Add the vegan fish sauce (if using), tamari or soy sauce and coconut sugar and simmer for a further 10 minutes or until reduced. If you'd like your curry to be really creamy, stir through the peanut butter. Remove from the heat and stir through the Thai basil leaves.

Serve with jasmine rice or rice noodles, and scatter over extra Thai basil leaves and sliced red chilli. Leftover curry paste will keep in an airtight container in the fridge for up to 1 week.

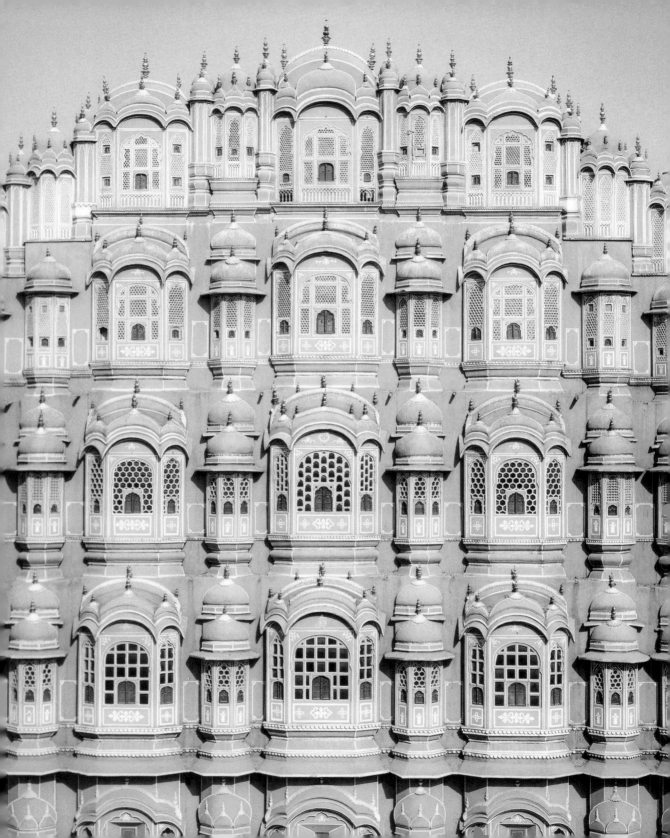

ALOO JEERA

Aloo jeera is a simple potato curry designed to be eaten alongside other Indian dishes. I love eating it with the chana masala on page 174 and the Indian eggplant curry on page 177. Scooped up with some homemade naan bread, it's what I call an impressive meal!

Serves 2
3 large potatoes
1 tablespoon avocado oil
1 long green chilli, deseeded and sliced
2–3 cm piece of ginger, sliced
2 teaspoons cumin seeds
¼ teaspoon ground turmeric
½ teaspoon ground coriander
½ teaspoon sea salt
1 tablespoon freshly squeezed lemon juice
chopped coriander leaves, to serve (optional)

Bring a large saucepan of salted water to the boil, add the potato and cook for 15–20 minutes or until just starting to soften. Drain and set aside until cool enough to handle, then peel and cut into 3 cm cubes.

Heat the oil in a large saucepan over medium–high heat. Add the chilli and ginger and sauté for 1 minute. Reduce the heat to medium, add the spices and salt and sauté for another minute. Stir through 3 tablespoons of water and add the potato to the pan. Increase the heat to high and sauté for 3 minutes or until the potato begins to crisp around the edges and turn golden.

Remove the pan from the heat and stir through the lemon juice. Scatter over the coriander leaves (if using) and serve with any of the Indian curries in this book as part of a shared meal.

CHANA MASALA

Chana (meaning chickpea) and masala (meaning curry) has to be my favourite Indian curry. During our time in India, we ate this curry with every meal. We shared other curries in order to try something new each time, but, in the end, the chana masala was always the best.

Serves 2

2 tablespoons avocado oil
1 onion, diced
400 g can whole tomatoes
400 g can chickpeas, drained and rinsed (see Tip)
2 teaspoons coconut sugar
2 tablespoons freshly squeezed lemon juice,
  plus lemon wedges to serve
sea salt
chopped coriander leaves, to serve
steamed basmati rice or Garlic Naan (see page 290),
  to serve

Masala curry paste

2–3 long red chillies, roughly chopped
3 garlic cloves, roughly chopped
2 teaspoons ground cumin
2–3 cm piece of ginger, roughly chopped
1 teaspoon ground turmeric
½ teaspoon sea salt
1 teaspoon black peppercorns
1 teaspoon garam masala
1 teaspoon ground coriander
1 teaspoon brown mustard seeds

Using a large mortar and pestle, pound the masala curry paste ingredients for about 10 minutes or until you have a smooth paste. (Alternatively, you can use a small food processor.)

Heat a saucepan over medium heat, add the oil and curry paste and sauté for 30 seconds. Add the onion and sauté for 2 minutes, then stir through the tomatoes and chickpeas. Reduce the heat to low and simmer for 30 minutes or until reduced to a thick curry.

Remove the pan from the heat, stir through the sugar and lemon juice, then taste and add a little salt, if necessary. Sprinkle the chana masala with coriander and serve with steamed basmati rice or garlic naan on the side and lemon wedges for squeezing over.

• •

TIP

Keep your chickpea liquid (aquafaba) to make the sriracha mayo on page 282 or the caesar dressing on page 110.

• •

INDIAN EGGPLANT
CURRY

This simple Indian curry is super delicious. I love the way the eggplant soaks up the curry sauce like a sponge as it's cooking. For some extra protein, you might like to add a can of chickpeas or make the chana masala on page 174 and serve them together. This is how we ate in India: an array of vegan curries served with rice and breads.

Serves 2

2 tablespoons avocado oil
1 onion, diced
2 dried curry leaves or bay leaves
300 g eggplant, cut into 2 cm cubes
400 g can whole tomatoes
sea salt
2 teaspoons coconut sugar
2 teaspoons freshly squeezed lemon juice
chopped coriander leaves, to serve
steamed basmati rice or Garlic Naan (see page 290), to serve

Eggplant curry paste

3 garlic cloves, roughly chopped
3 long red chillies, roughly chopped
2–3 cm piece of ginger, roughly chopped
½ teaspoon ground turmeric
1 teaspoon ground cumin
2 teaspoons yellow mustard seeds
1 teaspoon garam masala
½ teaspoon sea salt

To make the eggplant curry paste, place the ingredients in a mortar and gently pound with a pestle for 10 minutes or until you have a smooth paste. (Alternatively, you can use a small food processor.) Set aside.

Heat the oil in a large frying pan over medium-high heat. Add the curry paste, onion and curry or bay leaves and sauté for 2 minutes or until fragrant. Add the eggplant and sauté for another 2 minutes or until it has soaked up some of the curry paste and taken on a red colour.

Stir through the tomatoes, a pinch of salt and 3 tablespoons of water, then reduce the heat to low and simmer for 15–20 minutes or until the sauce has reduced and the eggplant is falling apart.

Remove the pan from the heat and stir through the sugar and lemon juice. Taste and season with extra salt if necessary. Sprinkle over a few chopped coriander leaves and serve with steamed basmati rice or garlic naan.

JACKFRUIT
ROGAN JOSH

Rogan josh is a spicy curry from the Kashmir region of India. It's typically made with lamb or goat, so it's not a curry I have actually tried, but after my travels in India I set out to experiment with my own vegan version. Instead of slow-cooked meat, I have used the versatile jackfruit. Its soft, stringy consistency is perfect for soaking up all that curry sauce.

Serves 3–4
2 tablespoons avocado oil
1 cinnamon stick
2 cloves
3 cardamom pods
2 dried bay leaves
1 onion, diced
1 carrot, diced
1 red capsicum, diced
400 g can young jackfruit, drained and rinsed, roughly chopped
3 tablespoons Coconut Yoghurt (see page 264) or coconut cream
chopped coriander leaves, to serve
steamed basmati rice or Garlic Naan (see page 290), to serve

Rogan josh curry paste
1 tablespoon finely chopped coriander stalks
2–3 cm piece of ginger, roughly chopped
3 garlic cloves, roughly chopped
2 red bird's eye chillies (deseeded if you prefer less heat)
1 teaspoon black peppercorns
2 teaspoons cumin seeds
1 teaspoon ground coriander
1 teaspoon sweet paprika
½ teaspoon sea salt
2 teaspoons garam masala
2 tablespoons tomato paste

To make the curry paste, place all the ingredients in a mortar and gently pound with a pestle for 10 minutes or until you have a smooth paste. (Alternatively, you can use a small food processor.) Set aside. If you are unsure about how much spice you can handle, leave out one of the chillies and add, to taste, when cooking.

Heat the oil in a large saucepan over medium–high heat. Add the cinnamon stick, cloves, cardamom pods, bay leaves and curry paste and sauté for 1 minute or until fragrant. Add the onion, carrot and capsicum and sauté for another minute, then add the jackfruit and 500 ml (2 cups) of water. Reduce the heat to medium–low, then cover and simmer for 30 minutes or until reduced.

Stir through half the coconut yoghurt or cream and simmer for a further 5 minutes.

Scatter over some coriander and serve with steamed basmati rice or garlic naan and the remaining yoghurt or cream on the side.

VEGGIE-LOADED LASAGNE

This vegan lasagne is a great dish to make when cooking for family or friends, or if you're wanting leftovers for the next day. Inspired by my travels in Italy, I have loaded this lasagne with the goodness of six vegetables!

Serves 6

360 g peeled and deseeded pumpkin,
  cut into 5 mm thick slices
1 eggplant, cut into 5 mm thick slices
1 zucchini, cut into 5 mm thick slices
1 teaspoon olive oil
80 g (2 cups) finely shredded kale leaves
150 g gluten-free pasta sheets
500 ml (2 cups) passata
1 cup basil leaves, shredded
½ × quantity Marinated Almond–Macadamia Feta
  (see page 270), mashed (optional)
micro herbs, to serve (optional)

Cauliflower sauce

350 g cauliflower florets
125 ml (½ cup) soy milk
1½ tablespoons nutritional yeast flakes
2 tablespoons tapioca flour
½–¾ teaspoon sea salt

Preheat the oven to 180°C fan-forced. Line a large baking dish with baking paper.

To make the cauliflower sauce, bring a saucepan of water to the boil, add the cauliflower and boil for 5–7 minutes or until cooked through. Drain and place the cauliflower in a blender with the remaining sauce ingredients. Blend until smooth, then set aside.

Heat a large non-stick frying pan over high heat. Working in batches, dry-fry the pumpkin, eggplant and zucchini for about 1 minute on each side to partially cook them. Remove from the pan and set aside.

Add the oil and kale to the pan, sauté for 1 minute, then set aside.

Lay pasta sheets in the base of the prepared dish (you'll need about three across the bottom) and top with one-third of the eggplant, passata, kale, zucchini, pumpkin and basil. Top with another layer of pasta and spread over one-third of the cauliflower sauce. Repeat this layering, spreading the almond–macadamia feta underneath the final layer of pasta (if using), and finish with a final layer of cauliflower sauce.

Bake for 50–60 minutes or until cooked through and bubbling. Allow to cool for 5 minutes before cutting. Serve with a few micro herbs sprinkled over the top, if desired.

FYSH & CHIPS

Here is my interpretation of an Aussie takeaway classic. This vegan version of fish and chips is inspired by a beer-battered tofu dish I ate at a seafood restaurant in Bali. I loved the idea of wrapping tofu in nori and battering it, which gave it a seafood flavour. I decided to use mushrooms instead of tofu and have added dried wakame to the batter for an even deeper fish flavour.

Serves 2

90 g (1½ cups) panko
    breadcrumbs
4 large flat mushrooms, cut into
    2–3 cm thick slices
2–3 nori sheets, cut into 4 cm
    wide strips
avocado oil, for shallow-frying
    (optional)
1 tablespoon finely chopped
    flat-leaf parsley leaves
sea salt and freshly ground
    black pepper
Tartare Sauce (see page 280),
    to serve
lemon wedges, to serve

Chips

3 all-purpose potatoes, cut into
    1.5 cm thick chips
2 teaspoons olive oil
1 rosemary sprig, leaves stripped
½ teaspoon sea salt

Batter

2 tablespoons dried wakame
    (see Tip) (optional)
1 tablespoon tamari or soy sauce
½ teaspoon baking powder
2 tablespoons tapioca flour
75 g (½ cup) plain flour
185 ml (¾ cup) soy milk

Preheat the oven to 180°C fan-forced. Line two baking trays with baking paper.

To make the chips, place the potato, oil, rosemary and salt in a bowl and toss well. Spread out on one of the prepared trays and bake for 30–40 minutes or until golden, crispy and cooked through.

Meanwhile, whisk all the batter ingredients in a bowl and put the panko breadcrumbs in a separate large mixing bowl.

Heat a large non-stick frying pan over high heat, add the mushroom and dry-fry the slices on each side for 45 seconds to soften them. Remove from the pan and place on paper towel to soak up any liquid.

Wrap each mushroom slice in a piece of nori and place on the second baking tray. Working with one piece at a time, dip a nori-wrapped mushroom in the batter, coating evenly, then transfer to the bowl of panko. Toss until evenly coated, then transfer back to the tray.

If you would like to bake your fysh, place the tray in the oven and cook for 30–40 minutes or until golden and crisp.

If you would like to fry your fysh, place a frying pan or wok over medium–high heat and add enough oil to cover the base of the pan by 5 mm. Test the oil is hot enough by dropping a breadcrumb into the hot oil – if it sizzles on contact, the oil is ready. Add half the fysh to the pan and fry for 3 minutes on each side or until golden. Transfer to a plate lined with paper towel. Repeat with the remaining fysh.

Sprinkle the parsley and a little salt and pepper over the fysh and serve with the chips, tartare sauce and lemon wedges on the side.

• •

TIP

You can purchase dried wakame from most Asian supermarkets, health-food stores or online.

PUMPKIN & MUSHROOM RISOTTO
WITH GARLIC & THYME

Pumpkin and mushroom risotto is a delicious and hearty meal that I often cook in advance when I know I've got a busy week coming up. I love experimenting with mushroom varieties, so I've used a mix of swiss brown, shiitake and oyster. Apart from the swiss browns, these mushrooms are typically found in Asian cuisine, but I wanted to try them in an Italian classic. If you can't find these varieties, use any mushroom that's available.

Serves 4

300 g deseeded pumpkin, skin left on, cut into 3 cm chunks
2 tablespoons olive oil
pinch of ground cinnamon
sea salt
1 litre vegetable stock
6 garlic cloves, crushed
330 g (1½ cups) arborio rice
125 ml (½ cup) white wine
5 thyme sprigs
200 g mixed mushrooms, such as swiss brown, shiitake and oyster, roughly chopped
3–4 large handfuls of baby spinach
freshly ground black pepper

Preheat the oven to 180°C fan-forced. Line a baking tray with baking paper.

Place the pumpkin on the prepared tray and toss through ½ teaspoon of the oil, the cinnamon and a pinch of salt. Bake for 30 minutes or until the pumpkin is soft and cooked through. Set aside.

Meanwhile, place the stock and 250 ml (1 cup) of water in a large saucepan and bring to the boil. Turn off the heat and cover.

Heat 1 teaspoon of the oil in another large saucepan over high heat. Add half the garlic and sauté for 30 seconds. Add the rice and white wine and cook, stirring, until the wine is absorbed. Add the thyme and 250 ml (1 cup) of the stock, then cover and cook, stirring occasionally, until the liquid is also absorbed. Continue to add the stock, stirring and waiting for it to be absorbed before adding more, until the rice is cooked through.

Meanwhile, heat the remaining oil in a frying pan over high heat. Add the remaining garlic and the mushroom and sauté for 5 minutes or until golden. Set aside.

When the risotto is almost ready, stir through the cooked mushroom and pumpkin and simmer for 3 minutes. Add the spinach and simmer for another minute. Season with salt and pepper, to taste, then spoon into bowls and serve.

VEGAN CHILLI

This chilli is the perfect soul warmer on a cold winter's night. It also tastes delicious for lunch or dinner the next day. With aromatic spices, corn chips to scoop up the chilli and creamy smashed avocado on top, it's my version of a Tex-Mex classic.

Serves 2 generously
1 teaspoon avocado oil
1 teaspoon ground cumin
1 teaspoon ground coriander
1 teaspoon smoked paprika
½ red onion, diced
2 garlic cloves, crushed
400 g can whole tomatoes
1 sweet potato, diced
1 red capsicum, diced
400 g can 3-bean mix, drained and rinsed
1 tablespoon chipotle sauce or sriracha chilli sauce
½ teaspoon chilli powder or 1 long red chilli, sliced
  (optional)
sea salt and freshly ground black pepper
1 avocado
juice of 1 lime, plus lime cheeks to serve

To serve
90 g (½ cup) cooked red or white quinoa
handful of coriander leaves
1 long red chilli, sliced
3 tablespoons Cheeze Sauce (see page 280)
100 g corn chips

Place the oil in a large saucepan over medium heat. Add the spices and sauté for 30 seconds, then add the onion and garlic and sauté for another 30 seconds.

Add the tomatoes, 125 ml (½ cup) of water and the sweet potato and bring to the boil. Cover and simmer for 6 minutes.

Add the capsicum and beans to the pan, then cover and simmer for 4 minutes. Add the chipotle sauce or sriracha chilli sauce and the chilli (if using), then season with salt and pepper. Continue to cook until the sweet potato is cooked through and the sauce has reduced and thickened.

Mash the avocado in a bowl with the lime juice and season with salt and pepper.

Divide the chilli between two serving bowls and top with the mashed avocado, cooked quinoa, coriander leaves and sliced chilli. Dollop over the cheeze sauce and serve with the corn chips and lime cheeks for squeezing over.

Mains

POKE BOWL

Originating from Hawaii but with a Japanese influence, poke is a deconstructed sushi roll that's much easier and less fiddly to make! This veggie-loaded poke bowl is inspired by one of my favourite lunch spots on the Gold Coast, Poke Poke on Mermaid Beach.

Serves 2
200 g firm tofu, cut into 2 cm cubes
300 g peeled and deseeded pumpkin,
   cut into 2 cm cubes
2 teaspoons olive oil
¼ teaspoon sea salt
¼ teaspoon ground cumin
110 g (½ cup) brown rice
1 avocado
1 tablespoon freshly squeezed lime juice
75 g (1 cup) finely shredded red cabbage
½ nori sheet, shredded

Zesty dressing
½ cup coriander leaves, plus extra to serve
2 tablespoons freshly squeezed lime juice
½ teaspoon sea salt
1 teaspoon apple cider vinegar
1 teaspoon coconut aminos
1 teaspoon olive oil

Crispy kale
80 g (2 cups) shredded kale leaves
1 teaspoon olive oil
¼ teaspoon sea salt

To serve (optional)
chilli powder
sriracha chilli sauce
sauerkraut

Preheat the oven to 180°C fan-forced. Line two large baking trays with baking paper.

Place the tofu and pumpkin separately on one of the prepared trays. Drizzle over the oil and sprinkle with the salt. Sprinkle the cumin over the pumpkin, then transfer the tray to the oven and bake for 25–30 minutes or until the tofu and pumpkin are golden and cooked through.

Meanwhile, cook the brown rice according to the packet instructions. Drain and set aside.

To make the dressing, place all the ingredients in a food processor and blend until smooth. Set aside.

To make the crispy kale, place the kale, oil and salt in a bowl and toss well to combine. Transfer to the other prepared baking tray and place on a low shelf in the oven. Bake for 4–5 minutes or until crispy – keep an eye on it as the kale can easily burn.

Mash the avocado with the lime juice in a small bowl and season with salt.

To construct your poke bowls, divide the rice between two bowls, pour over half the dressing and stir through. Top with the red cabbage, tofu, pumpkin, avocado, crispy kale, nori and the remaining dressing. If you like, finish with a few coriander leaves and a pinch of chilli powder, and serve with some sriracha chilli sauce and a spoonful of sauerkraut.

HEARTY LENTIL BOLOGNESE

This dish not only reminds me of Italy, it's also reminiscent of my childhood when spaghetti bolognese was a regular in our household. Here, I've created a hearty bolognese with lentils, TVP (textured vegetable protein) and loads of veggies, so it's packed full of plant protein and goodness.

Serves 4

2 teaspoons olive oil
1 onion, finely chopped
2 garlic cloves, finely chopped
1 red capsicum, chopped
400 g can chopped tomatoes
400 g can lentils, drained and rinsed
3 tablespoons TVP (textured vegetable protein) (optional)
1 tablespoon balsamic vinegar
5 swiss brown mushrooms, chopped
sea salt
300 g spaghetti (or konjac noodles, rice noodles or black bean pasta)
2 tablespoons chopped flat-leaf parsley leaves
freshly ground black pepper
grated vegan cheese, to serve

Garlic bread

small handful of flat-leaf parsley leaves
3 garlic cloves
1 tablespoon olive oil
pinch of sea salt
4 slices sourdough

Heat the oil in a large frying pan over medium–high heat. Add the onion and sauté for 30 seconds, then add the garlic and capsicum and sauté for another 30 seconds. Stir through the tomatoes, lentils, TVP (if using), balsamic vinegar, mushroom and 250 ml (1 cup) of water. Reduce the heat to medium–low and simmer for 20 minutes or until reduced, then season to taste with salt.

Meanwhile, preheat the oven to 180°C fan-forced.

Bring a large saucepan of salted water to the boil and cook the spaghetti according to the packet instructions.

To make the garlic bread, use a mortar and pestle to pound the parsley, garlic, oil and salt to make a paste. Spread the paste onto the sourdough slices, then place on a baking tray and bake for 5 minutes or until golden.

Drain the spaghetti and divide among serving bowls. Spoon the bolognese over the top and scatter over the parsley. Season with salt and pepper, sprinkle over some grated vegan cheese and serve with the garlic bread on the side.

SWEETS

CHAI-SPICED COOKIES

My favourite baked treat is a cookie, and these chai-spiced cookies are the perfect afternoon bite with a cup of tea. During my trip to India, I would often order soy chai tea and Indian sugar cookies, so when I came home I created this recipe to marry those flavours. Feel free to double the quantities to make a bigger batch.

Makes 8
55 g (½ cup) besan (chickpea flour)
85 g (½ cup) brown rice flour
65 g tapioca flour
2 tablespoons arrowroot powder
1 teaspoon bicarbonate of soda
¼ teaspoon sea salt
1 teaspoon ground cinnamon
½ teaspoon ground cardamom
75 g (⅓ cup) coconut sugar
1 teaspoon vanilla extract
1 tablespoon almond or soy milk
80 ml (⅓ cup) chilled coconut oil
4 drops of liquid stevia (optional)

To serve (optional)
sea salt flakes
dehydrated rose petals

Preheat the oven to 160°C fan-forced. Line a baking tray with baking paper.

Sift the flours, arrowroot powder, bicarbonate of soda, salt, cinnamon and cardamom into a large bowl and mix well.

Place the coconut sugar, vanilla, almond or soy milk, coconut oil and stevia (if using) in a separate bowl. Using a hand-held mixer, begin to beat on low speed, then increase the speed to medium as the ingredients come together. Continue to mix until the ingredients are well combined and the sugar has begun to dissolve into the coconut oil.

Add the wet ingredients to the dry ingredients and mix with your hands until a dough forms. Roll the dough into eight even-sized balls and place them on the prepared tray, allowing enough room for them to spread. Gently flatten with the back of a fork to make a pretty indentation.

Bake for 15–25 minutes or until golden, then transfer to a wire rack to cool. Sprinkle with salt flakes and dehydrated rose petals, if desired, and enjoy with a cup of tea.

Sweets

LAMINGTONS

Although there is some debate over whether the lamington originates from Australia or New Zealand, we all agree that this sponge cake dunked in chocolate and rolled in coconut is absolutely deeeelicious!

Makes 8

1 tablespoon flaxseed meal
140 g (1 cup) self-raising spelt flour
150 g (1 cup) plain flour
¼ teaspoon sea salt
1 teaspoon baking powder
3 tablespoons pure maple syrup
3 tablespoons olive oil
250 ml (1 cup) soy milk
150 g vegan dark chocolate, broken into pieces
60 g (1 cup) shredded coconut

Preheat the oven to 180°C fan-forced. Line a 20 cm × 15 cm baking tin with baking paper.

Place the flaxseed meal and 3 tablespoons of water in a bowl and set aside for 10 minutes.

Sift the flours, salt and baking powder into a bowl and stir to combine.

Pour the maple syrup, oil and soy milk into the flaxseed meal mixture and mix well, then add to the dry ingredients and fold together until just combined to form a smooth batter. Transfer to the prepared tin and bake for 40 minutes or until a skewer inserted into the centre of the cake comes out clean. Remove from the oven and set aside to cool completely.

Melt the chocolate in a heatproof bowl set over a saucepan of simmering water (don't let the bowl touch the water or the chocolate will seize). Carefully remove from the heat and set aside.

Cut the cake into eight even-sized pieces (you can trim the edges to make them square, if you like). Place the coconut in a shallow bowl.

To coat, dip each side into the melted chocolate and allow the excess to drip off. Transfer to the bowl of coconut and gently roll until each lamington is completely coated.

Store in an airtight container in the fridge for up to 1 week.

ANZAC BISCUITS

Anzac biscuits are another Aussie and New Zealand favourite. The name dates back to WWI, when women baked and sent these long-lasting treats to the ANZAC soldiers fighting the war abroad. They also happen to be my husband Alex's favourite, so I love baking them for him.

Makes 12
120 g (1 cup) spelt flour
1 tablespoon tapioca flour
¼ teaspoon sea salt
100 g (1 cup) rolled oats
60 g (1 cup) shredded coconut
80 ml (⅓ cup) coconut nectar
80 ml (⅓ cup) olive oil
5 drops of liquid stevia (optional)

Preheat the oven to 170°C fan-forced. Line a baking tray with baking paper.

Sift the flours and salt into a large mixing bowl. Add the oats and coconut and mix well.

Heat the coconut nectar and olive oil in a saucepan over medium heat. Bring to a gentle simmer, stirring, then remove from the heat and pour into the dry ingredients. Add the stevia (if using) and 2 tablespoons of water and mix to form a dough.

Roll the dough into 12 even-sized balls and place on the prepared tray. Gently flatten to about 1.5 cm thick, leaving room for spreading.

Bake for 12 minutes or until golden. Allow to cool for 30 minutes, then transfer to an airtight container and store in the pantry for up to 3 days.

CHOCOLATE & ROASTED MACADAMIA SLICE

This recipe is inspired by the macadamias that grow around northern New South Wales where I grew up. These nuts are really high in good fats, so I find just a small serving makes me feel really satisfied. This slice reminds me of a treat I used to eat called maca-bites, which my best friend's dad made at his cafe.

Makes 8 slices or 16 squares
320 g (2 cups) raw macadamias
2 tablespoons pure maple syrup
pinch of sea salt
55 g (1 cup) coconut flakes
180 g medjool dates, pitted
1 tablespoon raw cacao powder
150 g vegan dark chocolate, broken into pieces

Preheat the oven to 150°C fan-forced. Line a baking tray and an 18 cm × 13 cm slice tin with baking paper.

Place the macadamias in a bowl and add the maple syrup and salt. Toss together, then transfer to the prepared tray and bake for 25–30 minutes or until roasted and golden.

Meanwhile, blitz the coconut flakes, dates and cacao powder in a blender or food processor to form a rough dough. Transfer to a bowl.

Place 120 g (¾ cup) of the roasted macadamias in the blender or food processor and pulse until roughly chopped. Return the dough to the blender and blend again until well combined with the macadamias. Press the mixture into the base of the prepared tin and scatter the remaining macadamias over the top.

Melt the chocolate in a heatproof bowl set over a saucepan of simmering water (don't let the bowl touch the water or the chocolate will seize). Carefully remove from the heat and drizzle the chocolate over the prepared slice.

Transfer to the fridge and allow to set for 1 hour. Cut into eight slices or 16 small squares and serve.

Store in an airtight container in the fridge for up to 10 days, if they last that long!

PORTUGUESE
CUSTARD TARTS

Portuguese custard tarts, or pastel de nata, are made with flaky pastry that's filled with cinnamon-infused custard and baked at a really high temperature until crisp and caramelised. They are one of my husband Alex's favourite treats, so on our travels to Portugal he indulged in them daily. We visited the famous Portuguese custard tart bakery in Lisbon, Pastéis de Belém, where you can watch the bakers make these pastries and learn the secrets of the trade. Of course, these are not vegan as they contain eggs and dairy, but don't worry, I have a vegan version covered! The pastry takes a bit of time to make, but you will be so impressed with the end result.

Makes 8

250 ml (1 cup) soy milk
pinch of ground cinnamon, plus extra for sprinkling
pinch of ground turmeric
2 tablespoons pure maple syrup
1 teaspoon vanilla extract
2 teaspoons vegan butter
2 tablespoons cornflour
tiny pinch of kala namak (Himalayan black salt)
   (for that eggy flavour – optional)
coconut sugar, for sprinkling

Pastry (see Tip, overleaf)

150 g (1 cup) plain flour, plus extra for dusting
   and rolling
¼ teaspoon sea salt
80 ml (⅓ cup) cold water
120 g vegan butter, softened

To make the pastry, sift the flour and salt into a large mixing bowl. Pour in the water and mix with a wooden spoon. The dough should be wet and sticky.

Transfer the dough to a clean and well-floured work surface. Dust a little flour over the top, then knead and roll in circular motions for 10 seconds to form a ball. Dust with a little more flour, then invert a bowl over the dough and allow it to rest for 15 minutes.

Remove the bowl and ensure the surface is still well-floured. Press out the dough to a 10 cm square, then roll and stretch it into a 3–5 mm thick square. Using a spatula, spread 40 g of the vegan butter over two-thirds of the square, leaving a 2.5 cm border around the edge. Grab the two corners of the unbuttered third and fold this third into the centre, then fold the other side over the top (like folding a letter).

Sprinkle more flour over your dough, then flip it over and sprinkle flour on the other side. Roll and stretch the dough back out to a 3–5 mm thick square, then repeat the buttering and folding process with another 40 g of the butter. Transfer the dough to a tray lined with baking paper and place in the fridge to chill for 10 minutes.

RECIPE CONTINUED OVER THE PAGE ▶

PORTUGUESE CUSTARD TARTS, CONTINUED

Place the dough back on the floured work surface and dust with more flour. Roll back out to a 3–5 mm thick square and spread the final 40 g of the butter over the dough, but this time spread it over the whole square and only leave a 2.5 cm border along the top edge. Dip your fingers in some water and wet this unbuttered edge, then, starting with the end closest to you, roll up the dough into a tight log.

Sprinkle more flour over the dough log, then cover with plastic wrap and place in the fridge for at least 2 hours or, preferably, overnight (yes, it's a labour of love, but it's going to be worth it!).

When the dough is ready, preheat the oven to the highest possible temperature.

Remove the dough from the plastic wrap and cut the log into eight even-sized pieces. Press the dough into the holes of a cupcake tin by placing a piece in the centre of a hole with the swirl facing up. Wet your thumb with cold water, then press your thumb into the pastry, forming a well. Begin to move your thumb in circular motions, spreading the dough across the bottom and up the side of the hole, working it into a bowl shape. Dip your thumb back in the water as you go and continue to spread the dough until it is 3–5 mm above the edge of the hole. Repeat this process with the remaining pieces of dough.

Now it's time to make your vegan custard! Place the milk, cinnamon, turmeric, maple syrup, vanilla and vegan butter in a saucepan over medium heat. Whisking constantly, slowly sift the cornflour and kala namak (if using) into the mixture until it just starts to thicken, then, still whisking constantly, remove from the heat, as the custard can begin to thicken rapidly.

Pour the mixture into your pastry shells until they are three-quarters full, then sprinkle with a little coconut sugar and a pinch of cinnamon.

Bake for 12–15 minutes or until the pastry is golden and the custard is starting to caramelise. Remove from the oven and allow to cool for 10–15 minutes before eating.

These tarts are best eaten fresh, but will keep in an airtight container in the fridge for up to 5 days. You can store the pastry in the freezer for up to 1 month.

• •

TIP

Make a double batch of pastry and freeze it in an airtight container for your next round of custard tarts!

• •

THAI-STYLE 'NUTELLA' & BANANA PANCAKES

This street-food delight is cooked on roadsides throughout Thailand and enjoyed by locals and hungry tourists alike. Thai pancakes are not vegan, so I endeavoured to make a dairy-free version that I could enjoy for breakfast. You can swap the plain flour for wholemeal if you like, but you won't achieve the smooth texture reminiscent of Thai pancakes. If you do choose to use wholemeal flour, you might need a splash more water or milk as the fibre in wholemeal flour absorbs more liquid.

Serves 2

2 tablespoons flaxseed meal
150 g (1 cup) plain flour
2 tablespoons glutinous rice flour
pinch of sea salt
435 ml (1¾ cups) soy milk
1 tablespoon olive oil, plus extra
   for pan-frying
2 tablespoons pure maple syrup
1 teaspoon vanilla extract
2 bananas, sliced
pinch of coconut sugar
⅓ cup Homemade 'Nutella'
   (see page 272)
3 tablespoons shredded coconut
handful of chopped hazelnuts

Place the flaxseed meal and 125 ml (½ cup) of water in a large bowl. Stir well to combine and set aside for 10 minutes.

Sift the flours and salt into a large mixing bowl.

Add the soy milk, oil, maple syrup and vanilla extract to the flaxseed meal mixture and whisk to combine. Pour this mixture into the dry ingredients and whisk to form a runny batter. Set aside to rest for 30 minutes.

Preheat the oven to 100°C fan-forced.

Heat a large non-stick frying pan over medium–high heat and drizzle in a little olive oil. Add 80 ml (⅓ cup) of the batter and swirl the pan quickly to form a thin circle. Cook for 1–2 minutes or until bubbles start to form on the surface and the underside of the pancake is golden, then flip over and cook for a further 30 seconds. Transfer to a heatproof plate and place in the oven to keep warm. Repeat with the remaining batter to make six pancakes.

Place another frying pan over medium–high heat, then add the banana slices and fry on each side for 30 seconds or until golden and caramelised. Remove from the heat and sprinkle over the coconut sugar.

To serve, place three banana slices on one side of each pancake, then fold over the other side and cut in half to make two triangles. Place the triangles on serving plates and top with the remaining banana slices. Drizzle over the homemade 'nutella' and sprinkle with the shredded coconut and chopped hazelnuts.

CHOCOLATE CHIP
COOKIES

Chocolate chip cookies are my ultimate weakness when it comes to baked goods and I especially love a freshly baked warm gooey cookie on a winter's night. A good chocolate chip cookie recipe is great to have on hand and I forgot to add one to my first cookbook, so after testing and trialling many different variations, I have come up with my best recipe yet! The addition of coffee gives it that bittersweet edge that makes it so delicious.

Makes 10–12
1 tablespoon flaxseed meal
3 tablespoons soy milk
80 g (⅓ cup) vegan butter
45 g (⅓ cup) coconut sugar
1 teaspoon vanilla extract
1 shot espresso (or 1 teaspoon instant coffee
   mixed with 2 tablespoons hot water)
225 g (1½ cups) plain flour
½ teaspoon baking powder
90 g (½ cup) vegan dark chocolate chips

Preheat the oven to 160°C fan-forced. Line a baking tray with baking paper.

Combine the flaxseed meal and soy milk in a bowl and set aside.

Place the vegan butter, coconut sugar and vanilla extract in a large mixing bowl. Using a hand-held mixer, beat on medium for 2–3 minutes or until soft and velvety. Stir through the coffee and flaxseed mixture, then sift in half the flour and all of the baking powder. Set your mixer to low and beat until the ingredients are well combined. Add the remaining flour and fold through, then add half the chocolate chips and knead into the dough.

Roll heaped tablespoons of the dough into 10–12 even-sized balls. Gently flatten the balls to about 1.5 cm thick and press a few chocolate chips into the top of each cookie.

Bake for 15 minutes or until golden. Allow to cool for 5 minutes before eating, as the chocolate will be very hot.

The cookies will keep in an airtight container in the pantry for up to 4 days or in the fridge for up to 1 week.

GLUTEN-FREE DATE
&
SWEET POTATO BUNDT CAKES

We ate so many delicious dates when we travelled through the Middle East, so after our trip I wanted to create a healthy, gluten-free date cake to share with you. The consistency of these cakes is dense and moist – a bit like a brownie – and I think they taste even yummier when chilled.

Makes 8

500 g sweet potato, peeled and cut into
  2 cm cubes
150 g medjool dates, pitted
½ teaspoon sea salt
3 tablespoons coconut oil
125 ml (½ cup) soy or almond milk
1 teaspoon vanilla extract
35 g (⅓ cup) besan (chickpea flour)
30 g tapioca flour
40 g (⅓ cup) raw cacao powder
1 teaspoon baking powder
vegan star sprinkles (see Tip) and dried edible
  flowers, to decorate

Icing

40 g cacao butter, melted
1 tablespoon pure maple syrup
2 teaspoons coconut oil, melted
2 tablespoons cashew butter
1 teaspoon tapioca flour
2 teaspoons soy or almond milk
pinch of sea salt

. . . .

TIP
Vegan sprinkles can be purchased online.

. . . .

Preheat the oven to 160°C fan-forced. Line a large baking tray with baking paper. Lightly grease eight mini bundt moulds (or use a cupcake tin).

Place the sweet potato on the prepared tray and bake for 30 minutes or until cooked through.

Meanwhile, place the dates, salt and 125 ml (½ cup) of water in a blender and blend until smooth.

Add the cooked sweet potato, along with the coconut oil, soy or almond milk, vanilla and 3 tablespoons of water. Blend until smooth.

Sift the flours, cacao powder and baking powder into a large bowl and pour in the date mixture. Gently fold the mixture until just combined, then spoon evenly into the mini bundt moulds or cupcake tin, leaving a 5 mm gap at the top.

Bake for 50–60 minutes or until a skewer inserted into the centre of the cakes comes out clean. Remove from the oven and cool for 25 minutes before removing from the moulds or tin and transferring to a wire rack to cool completely.

To make the icing, place all the ingredients in a bowl and mix until smooth. Drizzle over the cooled cakes, decorate with the sprinkles and dried flowers and place in the fridge for 10 minutes to set before eating. The cakes will keep in an airtight container in the fridge for up to 5 days.

PEANUT BUTTER
CRACKLE SLICE

A decadent slice that will keep you coming back for more! This is a really quick dessert to whip up and store in the freezer for when you want a little treat. Inspired by the LCM bars we ate growing up, this slice has a delicious peanut butter twist.

Makes 12
250 g (1 cup) natural peanut butter
5 medjool dates, pitted
¼ teaspoon sea salt
3 tablespoons melted coconut oil,
  plus extra if needed
60 g (2 cups) puffed rice
40 g (⅓ cup) dried cranberries
60 g (1 cup) shredded coconut
265 g (1½ cups) vegan dark chocolate chips
3 tablespoons coconut flakes

Line a 26 cm × 18 cm baking dish with baking paper.

Place the peanut butter, dates, salt and coconut oil in a blender and blend until smooth.

Transfer to a large mixing bowl and fold through the puffed rice, cranberries and shredded coconut. Spread the mixture into the prepared dish and flatten with a spatula.

Melt the chocolate chips in a heatproof bowl set over a saucepan of simmering water, stirring until melted and smooth (don't let the bowl touch the water or the chocolate will seize). If the chocolate chips are struggling to melt, stir through 1–2 tablespoons of coconut oil. Spread the melted chocolate over the slice and sprinkle the coconut flakes over the top.

Place in the freezer for 1–2 hours to set, then slice into 12 pieces.

The slice will keep in an airtight container in the fridge for up to 2 weeks.

MANGO STICKY RICE

Mango sticky rice is my favourite Thai dessert and you can buy it at street-food stalls for as little as $1. Made with coconut milk, sugar and fresh mangoes, not only is it delicious, it's also vegan! I learned how to make mango sticky rice in Thailand, but I was pretty shocked at how much sugar was added. Here, I've made a healthier version; so healthy, in fact, that this dessert can also double as a breakfast recipe. You can even omit the coconut sugar or maple syrup altogether, if you don't like to have added sugar in your breakfast.

Serves 2
90 g (½ cup) glutinous rice, soaked in
   cold water overnight
sea salt
2 teaspoons coconut sugar or pure maple syrup
125 ml (½ cup) coconut milk
2 tablespoons crushed unsalted peanuts
2 tablespoons toasted coconut flakes
1 mango, diced or sliced
3 tablespoons Coconut Yoghurt (see page 264)
   or use store-bought, to serve
2 teaspoons coconut nectar or coconut sugar,
   to serve (optional)

Drain the rice and place in a saucepan with 375 ml (1½ cups) of water and a pinch of salt. Place over medium–high heat and bring to the boil, then reduce the heat to low and simmer for 10 minutes or until the rice is cooked through and the water has been absorbed.

Stir through the coconut sugar or maple syrup, coconut milk and ¼ teaspoon of salt and bring to the boil. Reduce the heat and simmer for 3–4 minutes, then remove from the heat and set aside to cool for 10 minutes.

Divide the sticky rice between bowls and top with the peanuts and coconut flakes. Serve with the mango and coconut yoghurt on the side and the coconut nectar or sugar on top, if desired.

Sweets

CHOC–CHILLI MANGO
HAYSTACKS

When I was in the United States, I came across chilli and lime–coated dried mango pieces in a local health-food store. They were so delicious, I decided to develop a chocolate recipe using a similar flavour combination.

Makes 6
120 g vegan dark chocolate, broken into pieces
80 g dried mango, finely sliced
60 g (1 cup) shredded coconut
pinch of coarse sea salt
1 teaspoon chilli flakes
1 tablespoon finely grated lime zest

Line a tray with baking paper.

Melt the chocolate in a heatproof bowl set over a saucepan of simmering water (don't let the bowl touch the water or the chocolate will seize). Stir until smooth, then carefully remove from the heat and set aside.

Combine the mango and coconut in a bowl, pour over the melted chocolate and stir to combine.

Spoon six small 'haystacks' of the mixture (about 3 cm in diameter) onto the prepared tray and sprinkle over the salt, chilli flakes and lime zest.

Place in the fridge or freezer for 15–20 minutes or until set and eat chilled.

The haystacks will keep in an airtight container in the fridge for 10 days.

PEANUT BUTTER
&
JELLY CHOCOLATE CUPS

These are like Reese's peanut butter cups, but even better! Not only are they sugar-free and keto-friendly, they're also easy to make and satisfy sugar cravings without giving you a sugar rush.

Makes 4 large or 8 small cups
40 g frozen raspberries
1 teaspoon chia seeds
100 g cacao butter, melted
3 tablespoons melted coconut oil
40 g (⅓ cup) cacao powder
3–4 teaspoons reishi mushroom powder (see Tips) (optional)
¼ teaspoon sea salt
1½ teaspoons liquid stevia or erythritol powder (see Tips) (or 3 teaspoons pure maple syrup)
2 heaped tablespoons smooth peanut butter

Crumble the raspberries into a small bowl and stir through the chia seeds. Set aside to thaw.

Combine the cacao butter, coconut oil, cacao powder, reishi powder (if using), salt and stevia or erythritol in a bowl and stir well. Spoon half the mixture into four large or eight small silicone cupcake moulds, stirring between each spoonful to prevent the reishi powder and sweetener settling on the bottom. Place the moulds in the freezer for 5–10 minutes to set.

Remove the moulds from the freezer and spoon an equal quantity of peanut butter in the centre of each mould. Using the back of a spoon, spread the peanut butter into a disc that is slightly smaller than the diameter of the chocolate base.

Next, spoon the raspberry 'jelly' on top of the peanut butter. Finally, spoon in the remaining chocolate mixture, ensuring the fillings are covered. Place in the freezer for another 5–10 minutes or until set.

The chocolate will quickly melt when the cups are removed from the freezer, so it's best to eat them straight away (see Tips). Once set, they will keep in an airtight container in the fridge for up to 1 week or in the freezer for up to 1 month.

• •

TIPS

If you would like a version that melts less quickly, replace the coconut oil with additional cacao butter as it has a higher melting point. They're very rich when made this way, so you may only need a half serving.

Reishi mushroom is popular in Eastern medicine. It's known for its immune-boosting properties and can be found in health-food stores and online.

Erythritol is a naturally derived sugar alcohol. It is unlikely to create the digestive issues that other sugar alcohols, such as sorbitol and xylitol, can cause. It can be found in health-food stores and some supermarkets.

DRINKS

HOMEMADE
COLD BREW

Cold brew is the latest coffee trend in Australia, and it's a great way to drink coffee when the weather is hot. The term 'cold brew' simply means coffee that's been infused without heat. It takes longer to brew than coffee made with boiling water, but the result is a smooth-tasting drink with softer, less bitter coffee notes.

Cold brew isn't a new method of making coffee. It dates back to at least 17th century Japan and iced coffee is regularly drunk throughout South East Asia. In Vietnam, it's made using hot water with a drip filter set over ice and condensed milk, but we didn't think it was as smooth as our cold brew back home in Australia. You don't need any fancy equipment to make this at home, just a big jar and a nut-milk bag or muslin cloth!

Serves 4
20 g coarsely ground coffee
1 litre filtered water
1 cinnamon stick (optional)
½ teaspoon vanilla powder (optional)

. . . .

TIP
Blend the cold brew with almond or coconut milk and pour over ice for a delicious iced latte, or serve with coconut condensed milk for a more authentic Vietnamese iced coffee.

. . . .

Place the coffee in a large glass jar and add the water. Stir well to combine and add the cinnamon stick and vanilla powder (if using).

Set aside to infuse in a cool place away from sunlight for 12–24 hours, stirring every 4–6 hours. The longer you leave it, the stronger the flavour will be.

Strain the cold brew through muslin or a nut-milk bag and discard the coffee granules. Drink straight away or store in the fridge for up to 5 days.

MEXICAN HORCHATA

I first tried horchata on my honeymoon in Mexico. It's a local drink made with soaked rice that's blended with spices and water, and the flavour reminds me of an iced chai, but with a subtle sweetness. Traditionally, horchata contains milk or milk powder, so here is my 'veganised' version. You may even like to throw in some sliced banana for a more filling, smoothie-like drink.

Serves 2

110 g (½ cup) brown rice, soaked in
    cold water overnight
250 ml (1 cup) almond milk
½ teaspoon vanilla extract
½ teaspoon ground cinnamon
1 teaspoon coconut sugar
3–4 drops of liquid stevia
1 cup crushed ice

Drain the rice and place in a blender with 250 ml (1 cup) of water. Blend for 1 minute on high, then strain the liquid through muslin or a nut-milk bag into a bowl.

Return the liquid to the blender and add the almond milk, vanilla, cinnamon, sugar and stevia. Blend on high until well combined, then pour over crushed ice and serve.

JAMU TONIC

Jamu is a traditional Indonesian tonic used for natural health and healing. It also happens to be delicious and extremely refreshing! Traditionally, jamu is made using good-quality honey, which is known for its antibacterial healing properties, so I've given it here as an option instead of the coconut nectar, but it's up to you to decide if you are comfortable consuming honey or not.

My best tips for finding ethically sourced honey are to track down a local beekeeper or honey producer, or even create your own home hive to help improve bee numbers. A lot of misinformation and generalisations are made about the honey industry, so I encourage you to research this topic in more depth. Planting flowers in your garden is the easiest way to help the bees!

Serves 2
2 cm piece of turmeric, peeled
5 cm piece of ginger, peeled
¼ teaspoon freshly ground black pepper
3 tablespoons freshly squeezed lime juice
1 tablespoon coconut nectar or ethically
   sourced local honey
ice cubes, to serve

Place all the ingredients and 125 ml (½ cup) of water in a blender and blend on high for 60 seconds. Add another 375 ml (1½ cups) of water and blend again for 30 seconds.

Strain through a fine sieve or nut-milk bag (but be aware that the turmeric will stain the bag).

Pour the tonic into ice-filled glasses or jars and enjoy. Any leftover tonic will keep in the fridge for up to 4 days.

MACADAMIA MANGO
SMOOTHIE

Like a mango Weis bar, but in a shake! This is what I imagine a true Australian summer drink to taste like: mangoes and macadamias blended into a dreamy smoothie. I've chosen salted roasted macadamias as not only do they taste delicious, they also add another level of flavour and bring out the sweetness in the mangoes.

I have included Kakadu plum powder as an optional addition to your smoothie. Kakadu plum is a native Australian ingredient from the north of Western Australia and the Northern Territory, where it's eaten as bush tucker and used as a traditional medicine by Indigenous communities.

Makes 1

250 ml (1 cup) macadamia or almond milk
140 g (1 cup) frozen mango cubes
3 tablespoons crushed salted roasted macadamias, plus extra to serve
2 ice cubes
1 teaspoon Kakadu plum powder (see Tips) (optional)

Blend all the ingredients in a blender until smooth. Pour into a glass or jar and top with extra crushed macadamias.

. . . .

TIPS

Kakadu plum powder can be found in some health-food stores and online.

If you would like to give your smoothie the ombre look in the picture, simply blend a fresh mango cheek with a dash of macadamia or almond milk and pour into a glass or jar. Then make the smoothie as instructed above and pour over the top.

. . . .

ISLAND SMOOTHIE

Papaya, dragon fruit, bananas and fresh coconut milk are accessible and cheap in Bali, so I was always using these tropical fruits in my smoothies when I lived there. Here, I've thrown some cashew butter into the mix to make this smoothie even creamier and more filling.

Serves 2

1 tablespoon desiccated coconut (optional)
1 teaspoon pure maple syrup (optional)
100 g frozen pink dragon fruit (see Tip)
100 g papaya, cut into cubes and frozen
1 banana, roughly sliced and frozen
1 tablespoon cashew butter
125 ml (½ cup) coconut milk
135 g (1 cup) ice cubes
2 cm piece of ginger (optional)
dried edible flowers, to serve (optional)

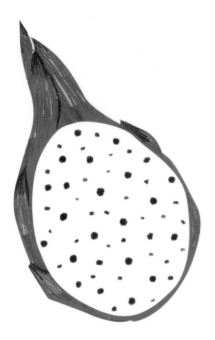

If you would like to decorate the rim of your glasses, place the coconut on a plate. Using your finger, rub the maple syrup around the rims of the glasses, then turn them upside down and dip the rims into the coconut.

Place the remaining ingredients except the edible flowers (if using) in a blender and blend until smooth.

Pour into the prepared glasses and scatter a few edible flowers over the top, if desired.

• •

TIP
Some supermarkets and health-food stores sell packets of frozen dragon fruit cubes. Look for them near the sachets of frozen acai and berries.

• •

Drinks

GINGERBREAD
TURMERIC SMOOTHIE

This smoothie is inspired by my trip to Lapland, where we visited Santa's village, made fresh gingerbread and played in the snow. It was minus 20 degrees in Finland, so we weren't drinking smoothies, but when I returned to Bali I decided to create a smoothie with gingerbread flavours. We also developed a plant-protein blend based on this flavour for our online store!

Makes 1
2 frozen bananas
½ teaspoon ground cinnamon
½ teaspoon ground ginger
½ teaspoon ground turmeric
1 tablespoon hemp seeds, plus extra to serve
1 tablespoon cashew butter
1 medjool date, pitted
250 ml (1 cup) almond milk
shredded coconut, to serve

Place all the ingredients in a blender and blend on high until smooth.

Pour into a glass or jar, sprinkle over some shredded coconut and hemp seeds and drink straight away.

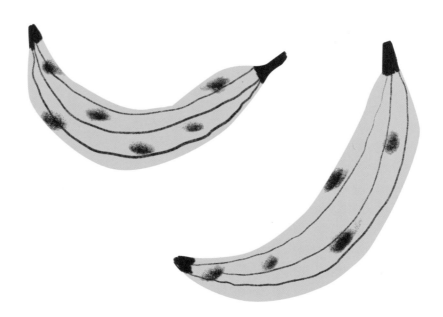

MIDDLE-EASTERN
SALTY DATE SHAKE

When we travelled through Oman and the UAE, hotels welcomed us with platters of dates and the breakfast bars often contained whole sections of this sweet fruit. Suffice to say, we ate our fair share of dates while we were there! One dish that stood out was a date and camel-milk shake, which of course I didn't try, but I loved the idea of creating a shake with dates to give sweetness and a slightly caramel flavour.

Makes 1
3–4 medjool dates, pitted
¼ teaspoon vanilla extract
pinch of sea salt
250 ml (1 cup) almond milk
4 ice cubes
1 tablespoon hemp seeds
Macadamia Granola (see page 29),
  to serve (optional)

Place all the ingredients in a blender and blend on high until smooth.

Pour into a glass or jar and sprinkle with a little granola, if you like.

PAPAYA & LIME
COCONUT SMOOTHIE

This is another tropical smoothie inspired by my time in South East Asia. Papaya is a fruit I've grown to love over the years and I particularly enjoy it with lime juice. If you're still on the fence about this fruit, do give it a try in this recipe, or simply swap the papaya for mango or dragon fruit.

Papaya contains the enzyme papain which assists with protein digestion, so you might like to add a tablespoon of plant-based protein powder or hemp seeds to pump up the nutrition.

Makes 1

1 tablespoon desiccated coconut
1½ tablespoons freshly squeezed lime juice, plus
  an extra lime wedge and a lime wheel, to garnish
160 g papaya, cut into cubes and frozen
125 ml (½ cup) coconut milk
125 ml (½ cup) coconut water or water
ice cubes, to serve

Place the desiccated coconut on a plate. Rub the rim of a glass or jar with the lime wedge, then turn the glass upside down and dip the rim in the coconut.

Place the lime juice, frozen papaya, coconut milk and coconut water or water in a blender and blend until smooth.

Fill your glass or jar with ice, pour the smoothie over the top and garnish with the lime wheel. Alternatively, you can blend the ice with the smoothie, but I prefer to leave it whole, so as not to dilute the flavour.

Drinks

PEANUT BUTTER SHAKE

This creamy shake feels like a treat when it's actually really nutritious. During our trip to India, we found this great little smoothie bar at an Indian airport making vegan peanut butter shakes. Funnily enough, I recall drinking one of these and playing ping-pong (yes, inside an airport!), and we ended up missing our flight for the first time ever.

Makes 1
2 frozen bananas
1 medjool date, pitted
1 tablespoon peanut butter, plus extra to serve
2 teaspoons raw cacao powder
250 ml (1 cup) almond milk
pinch of sea salt
shredded coconut, to serve
cacao nibs, to serve

Place all the ingredients in a blender and blend on high until smooth.

Pour into a glass or jar and top with an extra drizzle of peanut butter, some shredded coconut and cacao nibs. Enjoy!

MUSHROOM-INFUSED HOT CHOCOLATE

This recipe was inspired by a winter trip to Finland. We were staying in these incredible glass-cubed hotel rooms in Lapland, where you could watch the auroras from your bed. The temperature outside was pushing below minus 30 degrees Celsius and there was snow as far as the eye could see. Sitting in fire-heated hot-tubs, we were greeted with delicious vegan hot chocolates – a memory I will forever cherish.

This drink is definitely not your average hot choccy! The melted dark chocolate gives it a really rich and creamy texture, making it thick and truly decadent.

Serves 2

3 tablespoons vegan dark chocolate chips
500 ml (2 cups) macadamia or almond milk
  (or any plant-based milk)
pinch of sea salt
1 teaspoon reishi mushroom powder (see Tip)
1 teaspoon pure maple syrup, or to taste (optional)
raw cacao powder, for dusting

Place the chocolate in a heatproof bowl set over a saucepan of simmering water (don't let the bowl touch the water or the chocolate will seize). Melt the chocolate, stirring occasionally, until smooth. Remove from the heat and set aside.

Heat the milk and salt in a saucepan over medium heat until just bubbling, but not boiling. Pour into a blender and add the melted chocolate, reishi powder and maple syrup (if using). Blend on high for 10–15 seconds, then pour into mugs and dust with cacao powder.

. . . .

TIP

Reishi mushroom is popular in Eastern medicine. It's known for its immune-boosting properties and can be found in health-food stores and online.

. . . .

SPICY WATERMELON
MARGARITA

Anyone who knows me or follows my Instagram account will know that I love a spicy margarita. I actually don't often drink, unless I'm out for a nice dinner with friends or family or it's a special occasion, but I felt this book wouldn't be complete without a sneaky margarita! I've used watermelon in this recipe for a refreshing twist. You can leave out the tequila and make a virgin margarita, if drinking isn't your thing.

Serves 2
500 g watermelon
90 ml tequila
100 ml freshly squeezed lime juice, plus an extra
   lime wedge and a lime wheel, to garnish
1½ tablespoons chilli flakes
200 g (1½ cups) ice cubes
1 tablespoon sea salt flakes
dried edible flowers, to garnish (optional)

Juice the watermelon in a juicer or chop it into cubes and blend down to a juice and strain through a sieve. You should have about 400 ml of juice.

Place the watermelon juice, tequila, lime juice, 2 teaspoons of chilli flakes and ice in a cocktail or protein shaker and shake vigorously for 1 minute.

Combine the remaining chilli flakes and salt on a plate. Rub the lime wedge around the rims of two glasses and dip the rims in the chilli salt.

Pour the margarita into the glasses and top with a sprinkle of edible flowers, if desired. Add a lime wheel to each glass for extra prettiness. Cheers!

• •

TIP

For a smoky version of this margarita, add 5 drops of liquid smoke to the cocktail shaker and shake with the other ingredients.

• •

SALTED CARAMEL
ESPRESSO MARTINI

An espresso martini is my second favourite cocktail after a margarita. I think this recipe is inspired by all of my travels combined, since I seek out a great espresso martini in every city I visit. If drinking isn't your thing, drop the vodka and have yourself a delicious iced latte!

Serves 2
80 ml (⅓ cup) coconut milk
3 tablespoons espresso (about 2 shots)
90 ml vodka (optional)
2–3 teaspoons vegan caramel sauce,
  plus extra to serve (see Tip) (optional)
pinch of sea salt
200 g (1½ cups) ice cubes
2 tablespoons desiccated coconut
coconut nectar, to serve
coffee beans, to serve

Place the coconut milk, espresso, vodka (if using), caramel sauce, salt and ice in a cocktail or protein shaker and shake vigorously for 2 minutes.

Place the desiccated coconut on a plate. Rub the rims of two glasses with coconut nectar and dip the rims in the desiccated coconut.

Pour the espresso martini into the glasses and decorate with a few coffee beans (and an extra drizzle of caramel sauce if you like it sweet!).

· ·

TIP

I bought my vegan caramel sauce from an online vegan store. It's mainly made with coconut nectar, so if you can't find the sauce just use this instead, as it has a delicious caramel flavour.

· ·

BASICS

VANILLA HEMP & MACA MILK

This recipe marries two of my favourite ingredients – hemp seeds and macadamias. They both contain lots of healthy fats, so I wanted to use them to create a new nut-milk blend. Enjoy!

Makes 750 ml
50 g (⅓ cup) hemp seeds, soaked in cold water overnight
50 g (⅓ cup) macadamias, soaked in cold water overnight
750 ml filtered water
pinch of sea salt
1 teaspoon vanilla extract
1–2 calcium tablets (see Tips) (optional)
4–5 drops of liquid stevia (optional)

Drain and rinse the hemp seeds and macadamias. Place in a blender with 500 ml (2 cups) of the water, the salt, vanilla and calcium tablets (if using). Blend on high for 60 seconds, then add the remaining water and the stevia (if using) and blend for 30 seconds.

Drain the milk through a fine muslin cloth or nut-milk bag (see Tips), then transfer to a clean 750 ml jar, seal and refrigerate for up to 1 week.

. . . .

TIPS

The calcium tablets are optional, but I recommend adding them as they help anyone following a plant-based diet meet their daily calcium requirements.

The leftover pulp can be added to smoothies, fresh bread, bircher muesli or veggie patties.

. . . .

HOMEMADE COCONUT
YOGHURT

Makes 400 ml
400 ml can coconut milk (organic, if possible)
2 probiotic capsules (see Tips)
2–3 drops of liquid stevia (optional)
1 teaspoon vanilla extract (optional)

. . . .

TIPS

You may like to reserve a little yoghurt as a starter for your next batch. This helps to speed up the process because it already contains active probiotics. Just add 3 tablespoons of yoghurt to the coconut milk mixture and stir through.

Look for probiotics without prebiotics added. You can find them in the fridge section at good chemists.

. . . .

Bring a large saucepan of water to the boil. Place a 500 ml preserving jar and a small wooden spoon in the water and boil for 10 minutes. Transfer to a drying rack and allow to completely air-dry.

Pour the coconut milk into a blender and blend for 10 seconds.

Pour the coconut milk into the sterilised jar. Stirring, empty the probiotic capsules into the milk and stir until completely dissolved.

Cover the jar with muslin cloth or a nut-milk bag and secure with an elastic band. Place in a warm spot away from direct sunlight for 2–3 days (this could be as short as 1 day in really warm climates).

Check on your yoghurt twice a day, giving it a stir with a sterilised spoon. It should begin to thicken and develop a slightly sour taste. The yoghurt is ready when it suits your taste preference.

Stir through the stevia and vanilla (if using), then seal with a sterilised lid and place in the fridge. The yoghurt will thicken further as it chills.

The yoghurt will keep for up to 1 week. It's fantastic served with fresh fruit and my macadamia granola on page 29.

CRISPY PUMPKIN SEEDS

I am a big fan of reducing food waste whenever possible. When we were in Mexico, I discovered this great little way to use up the pumpkin seeds that I was otherwise discarding from my pumpkins. These crispy seeds are a great crunchy condiment to sprinkle on any savoury dish!

Makes ⅓ cup

⅓ cup fresh pumpkin seeds
  (scraped from the inside of a pumpkin)
2 teaspoons olive oil
½ teaspoon sea salt

Preheat the oven to 180°C fan-forced.

Don't wash the pumpkin seeds, as the gooey, stringy pumpkin will help them to caramelise. Place the seeds in a small baking dish and add the oil and salt. Toss together and bake for 10–15 minutes or until golden and crispy.

Allow to cool, then sprinkle over any savoury dish or eat as a snack. The pumpkin seeds will keep in an airtight container in the pantry for up to 1 week.

PARMESAN CRUMBLE

This simple savoury crumble is wonderful sprinkled over pasta dishes and bakes.

Makes about 1 cup

50 g (⅓ cup) cashews
⅓ cup nutritional yeast flakes
1 tablespoon hemp seeds
½ teaspoon sea salt flakes

Place the ingredients in the small bowl of a food processor and pulse 4–5 times or until the cashews have broken down to a rough crumble.

Store in an airtight container in the fridge for up to 1 month.

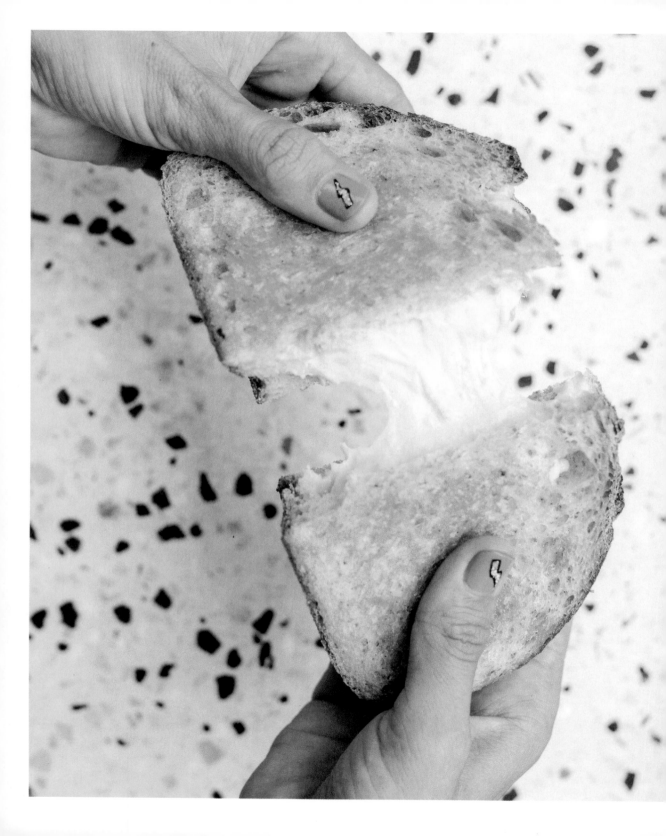

VEGAN MOZZARELLA

I accidentally discovered this recipe while trying to master banh xeo (see page 154). I replaced the rice flour with glutinous rice flour, poured it into a pan and ended up with a very sticky, stretchy mozzarella texture!

Serves 4
90 g (½ cup) glutinous rice flour
1 tablespoon nutritional yeast flakes
½ teaspoon sea salt
125 ml (½ cup) almond or soy milk

Place all the ingredients in a small saucepan over medium heat and whisk constantly for about 1½ minutes or until the mixture starts to thicken.

Remove the pan from the heat when nearly all the liquid has evaporated and keep stirring until the mixture is thick and the remaining liquid has disappeared. The mixture should have a melted cheese consistency. Transfer the 'mozzarella' to a bowl and use wherever a recipe calls for regular mozzarella.

Alternatively, you can fry the mozzarella by pouring a thin layer into a non-stick frying pan over medium heat. Fry until bubbles start to appear on the surface and the edges become golden, then remove from the heat, cut into slices and serve on toast or in burgers.

Vegan mozzarella doesn't keep well, so it's best to use it the same day it is made.

MARINATED
ALMOND–MACADAMIA FETA

This recipe builds on the baked herby almond feta in my first cookbook, except the macadamias make this feta even creamier! I especially love adding it to salads and Buddha bowls.

Makes 1 × 500 ml jar
155 g (1 cup) blanched almonds, soaked in cold water overnight
35 g roasted macadamias, soaked in cold water overnight
3 tablespoons olive oil, plus extra to fill the jar
3 tablespoons freshly squeezed lemon juice
½ teaspoon sea salt
1 tablespoon nutritional yeast flakes
3 rosemary sprigs
1 teaspoon black peppercorns
peel of 1 lemon

Line a 20 cm × 10 cm loaf tin with plastic wrap or baking paper.

Drain and rinse the almonds and macadamias, then transfer to a high-speed blender and add the olive oil, lemon juice, salt, nutritional yeast and 3 tablespoons of water. Blend on high for about 10 minutes, stopping every now and then to scrape down the sides of the blender. The mixture should be really thick and completely smooth by the end of the blending.

Transfer to the prepared tin and press down using a spatula. Refrigerate for 1–2 hours or until set.

Remove the feta from the tin and cut into 1.5 cm thick slices. Carefully place in a clean 500 ml jar and add the rosemary sprigs, peppercorns and lemon peel in the gaps between the feta slices.

Pour in enough olive oil to fill the jar, then seal and place in the fridge. The feta will keep for up to 1 week.

VEGAN 'NUTELLA'

Unfortunately, most store-bought hazelnut and chocolate spreads are not vegan and often contain large amounts of sugar. This healthy version can be spread on toast, drizzled over crepes, added to smoothies or spread on rice cakes, just like the original! It is also great with my Thai-style banana pancakes (see page 212).

Makes 500 ml (2 cups)

140 g (1 cup) hazelnuts, soaked in cold water overnight
80 ml (⅓ cup) coconut nectar
250 ml (1 cup) coconut milk
¼ teaspoon sea salt
1 teaspoon vanilla extract
3 tablespoons raw cacao powder
3 tablespoons cacao butter

Preheat the oven to 160°C fan-forced. Line a baking tray with baking paper.

Drain and rinse the hazelnuts. Transfer to the prepared tray and roast for 15 minutes or until they are dry and the skins are peeling off. Set aside to cool.

Place the hazelnuts in a tea towel and gently rub to remove the skins.

Transfer the hazelnuts to a high-speed blender along with the remaining ingredients and blend until smooth. Transfer to an airtight container and store in the fridge for up to 2 weeks.

VEGAN FISH SAUCE

Fish sauce is such a key ingredient in Asian cuisine, adding a salty punch to dishes and dipping sauces. This recipe will become your go-to fish sauce alternative, and the best part is that you don't need to use much, so the bottle will last a long time!

Makes 550 ml
80 ml (⅓ cup) tamari or soy sauce
3 tablespoons coconut sugar
2 teaspoons sea salt
2 teaspoons dried wakame (see Tip)
1 tablespoon white miso paste
1 tablespoon rice wine vinegar
1 dried shiitake mushroom, sliced
2 garlic cloves, crushed (optional)

• •

TIP

The dried wakame is essential in this recipe, as it gives the sauce that deep umami flavour. You can purchase dried wakame from most Asian supermarkets, health-food stores or online.

• •

Place all the ingredients and 435 ml (1¾ cups) of water in a saucepan over high heat. Bring to the boil, then turn off the heat and leave to cool for 30 minutes.

Meanwhile, bring a large saucepan of water to the boil. Carefully place a large bottle or jar in the water and boil for 10 minutes. Transfer to a drying rack and allow to completely air-dry.

Strain the fish sauce into the sterilised bottle or jar or leave the mushroom and wakame in to continue to infuse for a stronger umami flavour.

The sauce will keep in the fridge for up to 2 months. Use as a replacement whenever a recipe calls for fish sauce.

FIERY KOREAN SAUCE

Serve this spicy sauce with bibimbap (see page 142), Korean sushi (see page 135) or spicy ramen (see page 120).

Makes 120 ml
3 tablespoons gochujang chilli paste (see Tips)
  or sriracha chilli sauce
2 garlic cloves, crushed
1½ tablespoons tamari or soy sauce
2 teaspoons sesame oil
1 teaspoon coconut sugar (optional)
1 teaspoon Vegan Fish Sauce (see page 275)
  (optional)

Mix all the ingredients and 1 tablespoon of water in a bowl, stirring until the sugar dissolves. Serve in ramekins alongside your favourite Korean dishes.

Store in an airtight container in the fridge for up to 2 weeks.

· ·

TIPS

For a milder sauce, only add 2 tablespoons of the chilli paste or sauce, an additional 1 tablespoon of water and 1 tablespoon of coconut sugar (the sugar will balance out some of the spice).

Gochujang chilli paste can be purchased from Asian supermarkets.

· ·

Basics

NUOC CHAM

This dipping sauce accompanies many Vietnamese dishes, such as banh xeo (see page 154), rice paper rolls (see page 79), spring rolls and dumplings. Traditionally made with fish sauce, this is my vegan interpretation.

Makes 250 ml (1 cup)
2 tablespoon rice wine vinegar
3 tablespoons Vegan Fish Sauce (see page 275)
2 tablespoons coconut sugar
1 long red chilli, finely diced (or use 1 bird's eye chilli if you like heat)
1 tablespoon crushed garlic
3 tablespoons freshly squeezed lime juice

Place the ingredients and 3 tablespoons of water in a jar or bowl and shake or stir to combine. Serve the nuoc cham alongside your favourite Vietnamese dishes.

Store in an airtight container in the fridge for up to 2 weeks.

RANCH DIPPING SAUCE

This creamy dipping sauce is zesty and delicious. Dill is my favourite herb and this sauce takes me back to the United States, where we tried buffalo cauliflower wings with an amazing ranch sauce.

Makes about 185 ml (¾ cup)
50 g (⅓ cup) cashews
3 tablespoons soy or almond milk
1 tablespoon freshly squeezed lemon juice
1 tablespoon nutritional yeast flakes
½ teaspoon sea salt
½ teaspoon garlic powder
½ teaspoon freshly ground black pepper
1 teaspoon apple cider vinegar
1 teaspoon pure maple syrup
1 tablespoon chopped dill fronds
3 chives, snipped, plus extra to serve

Place all the ingredients except the herbs in a blender with 2 teaspoons of water and blend until smooth. Add the dill and chives and pulse for 5 seconds, so that the herbs are still visible.

Transfer to a small bowl and garnish with extra snipped chives. Serve with my cauliflower buffalo wings on page 66 or use as a salad dressing.

Leftover sauce can be stored in an airtight container in the fridge for up to 5 days.

TARTARE SAUCE

This delicious sauce goes really well with my fysh and chips on page 185 and the salt and pepper kalamari on page 88. It's also great slathered on burgers or served as a dip.

Makes about 250 g (1 cup)
80 g (½ cup) cashews
1 tablespoon olive oil
1½ tablespoons freshly squeezed lemon juice
1 garlic clove
1 teaspoon apple cider vinegar
¼ teaspoon sea salt
1 teaspoon dijon mustard
1 tablespoon chopped dill fronds, plus extra to serve
1 teaspoon capers, drained and rinsed

Place the cashews, olive oil, lemon juice, garlic, apple cider vinegar, salt, mustard and 125 ml (½ cup) of water in a blender and blend on high until smooth and creamy.

Add the dill and capers and pulse a few times until combined – you still want to see some green.

Transfer to a small bowl to serve and top with some extra chopped dill fronds. Store in an airtight container in the fridge for up to 5 days.

CHEEZE SAUCE

This Mexican-style cheeze sauce is awesome on nachos and as a dip for corn chips or fries, and it has the added goodness of potatoes and carrots!

Makes 300 ml
1 small potato, peeled and cut into 2 cm cubes
½ carrot, cut into 2 cm cubes
50 g (⅓ cup) cashews (omit for a nut-free sauce)
3 tablespoons nutritional yeast flakes
½ teaspoon garlic powder
1 teaspoon onion powder
½ teaspoon ground cumin
½ teaspoon smoked paprika, plus extra to serve
2–4 teaspoons chipotle sauce
½ teaspoon sea salt
1 teaspoon apple cider vinegar

Bring a small saucepan of salted water to the boil, add the potato and boil, covered, for 5 minutes. Add the carrot and continue to boil for a further 5 minutes or until the vegetables are soft. Drain and transfer to a blender.

Add the remaining ingredients to the blender, along with 80 ml (⅓ cup) of water, and blend until smooth and creamy.

Transfer to a bowl and sprinkle over a little extra smoked paprika. This sauce is great on nachos, tacos, Mexican salads, with baked potato chips, as a dip or whenever a cheese sauce is required.

Leftover sauce will keep in an airtight container in the fridge for up to 3 days.

Tartare sauce

Cheeze sauce

Ranch dipping sauce (recipe previous page)

SRIRACHA MAYO

This spicy mayo is a great way to use the liquid from your canned chickpeas! It may sound kinda funky, but it's a key ingredient for achieving that silky mayo texture. I love to serve this with the banh mi on page 166 and the jackfruit dumplings on page 75.

Makes 300 ml
100 g (⅔ cup) cashews, soaked in cold water overnight
185 ml (¾ cup) aquafaba (liquid from a 400 g can chickpeas)
1 tablespoon nutritional yeast flakes
½ teaspoon sea salt
3 tablespoons olive oil
2 tablespoons sriracha chilli sauce
1 garlic clove

Drain the cashews and place in a blender along with the rest of the ingredients. Blend on high for 1 minute or until you have a smooth, creamy mayo.

Transfer to a jar, seal and store in the fridge for up to 1 week.

CASHEW CREAM CHEESE

Cashew cream cheese is a true vegan staple. I use this in place of sour cream on nachos and tacos, as a mayo on burgers and as a delicious pizza topping. Leftovers are wonderful on salads, baked veggies or as a dip for veggie sticks. Nutritional yeast is the key ingredient to getting that cheesy flavour. Most nutritional yeast flakes are fortified with vitamin B12, an important nutrient that's only found in animal products.

Makes about 500 g (2 cups)
230 g (1½ cups) cashews, soaked in cold water overnight
1 teaspoon garlic flakes
1 tablespoon apple cider vinegar
3 tablespoons nutritional yeast
¼ teaspoon sea salt
juice of 1 lemon

Drain the cashews and transfer to a food processor or blender with the rest of the ingredients and 3 tablespoons of water. Blend until smooth and creamy, adding extra water (in 3 tablespoon increments) until the mixture reaches the desired consistency.

Store in an airtight container in the fridge for up to 5 days.

SPICY KOREAN KIMCHI

Kimchi is a traditional Korean side dish made with fermented cabbage. Most varieties of kimchi contain shrimp paste and fish sauce, so here I have tried to create an authentic-tasting vegan version that will fire up the belly! When I visited Seoul, I loved learning about the flavour variations of different kimchi, but the spicy version is still my favourite. Rich in probiotics, kimchi is a great accompaniment to any dish, but especially the bibimbap recipe on page 142.

Makes 1 × 1.5 litre jar
½ wombok
2 teaspoons sea salt
3 tablespoons Vegan Fish Sauce (see page 275)
½ cup gochujang chilli paste (see Tips) or 3 tablespoons chilli powder
2 tablespoons coconut sugar
6 garlic cloves, crushed
3 cm piece of ginger, finely sliced
1 carrot, julienned
1 onion, finely sliced

. . . .

TIPS

In warmer, more tropical climates, kimchi can ferment in as little as 2–3 days. In cooler climates, it may take up to 1 week.

Gochujang chilli paste can be purchased from Asian supermarkets.

. . . .

Before you begin, thoroughly clean your work surface, knife, a large mixing bowl and your hands to prevent possible bad bacteria getting into your fermentation, which can make it go rancid.

Bring a large saucepan of water to the boil. Carefully place a 1.5 litre preserving jar (or 2 × 700 ml, or 3 × 500 ml jars) and a pair of tongs in the water and boil for 10 minutes. Transfer to a drying rack and allow to completely air-dry.

Remove the bottom 1–2 cm of the cabbage and discard. Chop the cabbage into long strips (about 2 cm × 5 cm) and place in the bowl. Sprinkle over the salt and mix with your hands, massaging the salt into the cabbage. Set aside for 30 minutes.

Meanwhile, combine the vegan fish sauce, gochujang or chilli powder, coconut sugar, garlic, ginger and 80 ml (⅓ cup) of water in a bowl. Set aside.

Massage the cabbage again and set aside for a further 30 minutes, then toss again – the cabbage should be soft and you'll see water leaching out. Strain this excess water by tossing the cabbage in a colander or sieve. Return the cabbage to the mixing bowl.

Wash your hands thoroughly again, then add the carrot, onion and fish sauce mixture to the cabbage. Massage the mixture into the vegetables to evenly coat.

Using the sterilised tongs, transfer your kimchi to the sterilised jar. Press the kimchi down to remove any air and to push the cabbage under the liquid, then firmly seal. Place in a warm spot away from direct sunlight for 3–7 days (the time will depend on your climate; see Tips). Check your kimchi daily to make sure it is fermenting – you should start to see bubbles rising to the top and it may make a fizzing sound. Release the gases by unscrewing the lid and ensure it's not going off. Push any air bubbles out using a sterilised chopstick or spoon, then reseal.

Your kimchi is ready when it has a slightly sour and tangy taste. The longer you leave it, the more sour and tangy it will become. Once it is to your liking, transfer the jar to the fridge to stop the fermentation process. The kimchi will keep for up to 2 months.

PICKLED VEG

Throughout my travels to Vietnam and Korea, I learned how to use crisp pickled veg in or alongside local dishes. Homemade pickled veg are so quick and easy to make, and so much better for you than the store-bought versions that were probably made 6–12 months ago and look devoid of any nutrients. You can pickle just about any veggies you like, either separately in their own jars or thrown in the same jar for simplicity.

Makes 1 × 1 litre jar
1 carrot, julienned
6 cm piece of daikon, cut into thick matchsticks
1 red onion, finely sliced
1 Lebanese cucumber, cut into 5 mm thick slices
1 long red chilli, cut into thin strips (deseeded for a milder flavour)
1 fresh jalapeño, sliced

Pickling liquid
250 ml (1 cup) apple cider vinegar
1 teaspoon sea salt
2 teaspoons coconut sugar (optional)

To make the pickling liquid, heat all the ingredients and 250 ml (1 cup) of water in a saucepan over medium heat. Bring to the boil, then remove from the heat and set aside to cool for 20 minutes.

Meanwhile, bring a large saucepan of water to the boil. Carefully place a 1 litre preserving jar (or 2 × 500 ml jars) and a pair of tongs in the water and boil for 10 minutes. Transfer to a drying rack and allow to completely air-dry.

Using the sterilised tongs, place all the vegetables in the jar and pour over the liquid. Seal the jar and transfer to the fridge. The pickled veg will be ready to eat after 2 hours, but will taste even better if left overnight. Store in the fridge for up to 2 weeks – they may keep for longer, but I prefer to use them within this timeframe to maintain the vitamin and mineral levels in the veg.

Add your pickles to sandwiches, burgers, salad bowls and tacos for a tangy and refreshing crunch.

Coconut bakon

Konjac bakon

Rice paper bakon

BAKON,
THREE WAYS

These vegan bacon substitutes are a fun way to add texture and saltiness to some of the dishes in this book. Each variation gives a different taste or texture, so it's really up to you to decide which is your fave!

Serves 4

Marinade
¼ teaspoon liquid smoke (see Tips)
2 teaspoons tamari or soy sauce
1 teaspoon pure maple syrup or coconut sugar
1 teaspoon olive oil
⅛ teaspoon sea salt
¼ teaspoon smoked paprika

Rice paper bakon
4 rice paper sheets

Konjac bakon
250 g (1 cup) konjac noodles (see Tips),
  cut into 2.5 cm lengths

Coconut bakon
55 g (1 cup) coconut flakes

• • • • • • • • • • • • • • • • • • • •

TIPS

Liquid smoke can be bought online or from specialty food shops.

You will find konjac noodles at most Asian supermarkets.

• • • • • • • • • • • • • • • • • • • •

Preheat the oven to 150°C fan-forced. Line a baking tray with baking paper.

Combine all the marinade ingredients in a large bowl.

To make the rice paper bakon, run the rice paper sheets under water for 2 seconds, then shake dry and place on a clean work surface. Transfer the sheets one at a time to the marinade and massage with your hands. Cut the sheets into 5 cm wide rectangles and transfer to the prepared tray.

To make the konjac or coconut bakon, add the konjac noodles or coconut flakes to the marinade and toss to coat. Transfer to the prepared tray.

Bake for 8–12 minutes, checking on your bakon regularly to make sure it doesn't burn.

Add to your favourite dishes or store in an airtight container in the fridge for up to 2 days.

GARLIC NAAN

Homemade naan bread is a much healthier alternative to store-bought naan, which is often filled with preservatives. Serve this delicious garlic naan with any of the Indian curries in this book.

Makes 6–8
2 teaspoons coconut sugar
7 g sachet active dried yeast
300 g (2 cups) bread flour, plus extra for dusting
1 teaspoon baking powder
sea salt
80 g (⅓ cup) Coconut Yoghurt (see page 264)
3 tablespoons olive oil
4 garlic cloves
1 teaspoon cumin seeds

Place 125 ml (½ cup) of warm water, half the coconut sugar and the dried yeast in a mixing bowl. Stir and set aside for 15 minutes or until the surface starts to foam.

Meanwhile, sift the flour, baking powder, ½ teaspoon of salt and the remaining coconut sugar into a large bowl.

Pour the yeast mixture into the dry ingredients and add the coconut yoghurt and 1 tablespoon of the olive oil. Mix to form a rough dough.

Turn out the dough onto a lightly floured surface and knead for 8–10 minutes or until soft and stretchy. Place in bowl, cover and rest for 1 hour or until the dough doubles in size.

While the dough is resting, place the garlic, cumin seeds, a pinch of salt and the remaining olive oil in a mortar and pound with a pestle to form a paste.

Divide the dough into six to eight even-sized pieces and roll into balls. Place on a lightly floured baking tray and cover with a damp tea towel.

Preheat the oven to 160°C fan-forced. Place a large non-stick frying pan over high heat.

Roll out the first ball to a 5 mm thick circle. Fry for 3 minutes, allowing it to puff up. Flip and fry for another 3 minutes or until charred spots appear. Repeat with the remaining dough.

Spread the garlic paste over the naan, then place directly on an oven shelf and bake for 5 minutes or until the garlic is just golden. Serve immediately.

CONVERSION CHART

Measuring cups and spoons may vary slightly from one country to another, but the difference is generally not enough to affect a recipe. All cup and spoon measures are level.

One Australian metric measuring cup holds 250 ml (8 fl oz), one Australian tablespoon holds 20 ml (4 teaspoons) and one Australian teaspoon holds 5 ml. North America, New Zealand and the UK use a 15 ml (3-teaspoon) tablespoon.

LENGTH

METRIC	IMPERIAL
3 mm	⅛ inch
6 mm	¼ inch
1 cm	½ inch
2.5 cm	1 inch
5 cm	2 inches
18 cm	7 inches
20 cm	8 inches
23 cm	9 inches
25 cm	10 inches
30 cm	12 inches

LIQUID MEASURES

ONE AMERICAN PINT	ONE IMPERIAL PINT
500 ml (16 fl oz)	600 ml (20 fl oz)

CUP	METRIC	IMPERIAL
⅛ cup	30 ml	1 fl oz
¼ cup	60 ml	2 fl oz
⅓ cup	80 ml	2½ fl oz
½ cup	125 ml	4 fl oz
⅔ cup	160 ml	5 fl oz
¾ cup	180 ml	6 fl oz
1 cup	250 ml	8 fl oz
2 cups	500 ml	16 fl oz
2¼ cups	560 ml	20 fl oz
4 cups	1 litre	32 fl oz

DRY MEASURES

The most accurate way to measure dry ingredients is to weigh them. However, if using a cup, add the ingredient loosely to the cup and level with a knife; don't compact the ingredient unless the recipe requests 'firmly packed'.

METRIC	IMPERIAL
15 g	½ oz
30 g	1 oz
60 g	2 oz
125 g	4 oz (¼ lb)
185 g	6 oz
250 g	8 oz (½ lb)
375 g	12 oz (¾ lb)
500 g	16 oz (1 lb)
1 kg	32 oz (2 lb)

OVEN TEMPERATURES

CELSIUS	FAHRENHEIT	CELSIUS	GAS MARK
100°C	200°F	110°C	¼
120°C	250°F	130°C	½
150°C	300°F	140°C	1
160°C	325°F	150°C	2
180°C	350°F	170°C	3
200°C	400°F	180°C	4
220°C	425°F	190°C	5
		200°C	6
		220°C	7
		230°C	8
		240°C	9
		250°C	10

THANK YOU

Creating a cookbook is a huge job and one that I couldn't have done without the help and encouragement of many people. I would like to personally thank those who have contributed in some form.

To my husband, Alex, thank you for your absolute help and support during the creation of this book. Not only have you been with me throughout all of the travels that inspired the recipes in this book, you also helped to test, try, re-test, cook, shoot and clean up every single recipe in this book! Our shoot weeks were absolute madness and I could not have done it without you.

To my sister and best friend, Lauren, thank you for inspiring me to travel and for supporting every project I work on. Many of the recipes in this book were inspired by travels with you and you are the most honest taste tester for my recipes!

To my wholesome community of followers, thank you for always supporting my recipes and business ventures, for inspiring me to continue to share my wholesome life, my wholesome recipes and my nutrition knowledge. I would not be here living my dream without you guys, so thank you so so much!

A special thank you to everyone who supported book number one! Publishing my first ever cookbook was a nerve-wracking experience, but with your support, *Elsa's Wholesome Life* became a bestselling cookbook and I was able to continue doing what I love, creating delicious plant-based recipes – and a second book!

To everyone I have met during my travels. Thank you to the street food vendors and cooking teachers who have shared their knowledge of local ingredients and recipes handed down through generations. Thank you to all the restaurants and cafes I have visited that have shaped recipes within this book. And lastly, thank you to all of the countries around the world that have allowed me to visit and experience their cultures and cuisines.

The Plum team

Mary Small, thank you for believing in me in not only making me a published author once, but again a second time! I cannot thank you enough for giving me these opportunities, it really is a dream come true.

Jane Winning, it has been such a pleasure to work with you on my second cookbook. Thank you for your support and patience throughout this process and for believing in my vision for it.

Arielle Gamble, my designer and illustrator, I'm so happy to have you back on my second book. Your beautiful design and illustrations have really tied *The Global Vegan* back to my first book and to my Elsa's Wholesome Life brand.

Lucy Heaver, my editor, thank you for being so excellent with words – you really have helped to improve the flow of my writing in this book.

Shoot locations

Thank you to Zoe Paul of Mister Zimi, Hannah Williams of Vacay Co and Yvonne Pretti of Beach Shack 4220 for generously allowing us to come and stay to shoot parts of this cookbook in your beautiful homes.

INDEX

Index

A PLUM BOOK

First published in 2019 by
Pan Macmillan Australia Pty Limited
Level 25, 1 Market Street,
Sydney, NSW, Australia 2000

Level 3, 112 Wellington Parade,
East Melbourne, Victoria, Australia 3002

Text copyright © Ellie Bullen 2019
Photography copyright © Ellie Bullen 2019
Design Arielle Gamble copyright © Pan Macmillan 2019

The moral right of the author has been asserted.

Design and illustrations by Arielle Gamble
Typesetting by Post Pre-press Group
Editing by Lucy Heaver
Index by Helena Holmgren
Photography by Ellie Bullen
Prop and food styling by Ellie Bullen
Food preparation by Ellie Bullen
Colour reproduction by Splitting Image Colour Studio
Printed and bound in China by Imago Printing International Limited

A CIP catalogue record for this book is available from the National Library of Australia.

All rights reserved. No part of this book may be reproduced or transmitted by any person or entity
(including Google, Amazon or similar organisations), in any form or means, electronic or mechanical,
including photocopying, recording, scanning or by any information storage and retrieval system,
without prior permission in writing from the publisher.

We advise that the information contained in this book does not negate personal responsibility on
the part of the reader for their own health and safety. It is recommended that individually tailored
advice is sought from your healthcare or medical professional. The publishers and their respective
employees, agents and authors are not liable for injuries or damage occasioned to any person as a
result of reading or following the information contained in this book.

10 9 8 7 6 5 4 3